The Excel Statistics Companion

Kenneth M. Rosenberg
SUNY—Oswego

THOMSON ™

WADSWORTH

Australia • Canada • Mexico • Singapore • Spain • United Kingdom • United States

THOMSON

WADSWORTH

Publisher: Vicki Knight
Assistant Editor: Jennifer Wilkinson
Editorial Assistant: Monica Sarmiento
Technology Project Manager: Darin Derstine
Marketing Manager: Lori Grebe
Marketing Assistant: Laurel Anderson
Advertising Project Manager: Brian Chaffee
Project Manager, Editorial Production: Candace Chen

Art Director: Vernon Boes
Print Buyer: Lisa Claudeanos
Permissions Editor: Sommy Ko
Text Designer: Brian May
Cover Designer: Laurie Albrecht
Cover Image: Guy Grenier/Masterfile
Cover and Text Printer: Webcom

Printed in Canada
1 2 3 4 5 6 7 07 06 05 04 03

For more information about our products, contact us at:
Thomson Learning Academic Resource Center
1-800-423-0563
For permission to use material from this text, contact us by:
Phone: 1-800-730-2214
Fax: 1-800-730-2215

Web: http://www.thomsonrights.com

Library of Congress Control Number: 2003115082

ISBN 0-534-64230-6

MICROSOFT® is a registered trademark, and EXCEL is a trademark of the Mirosoft Corporation.

Wadsworth/Thomson Learning
10 Davis Drive
Belmont, CA 94002-3098
USA

Asia
Thomson Learning
5 Shenton Way #01-01
UIC Building
Singapore 068808

Australia/New Zealand
Thomson Learning
102 Dodds Street
Southbank, Victoria 3006
Australia

Canada
Nelson
1120 Birchmount Road
Toronto, Ontario M1K 5G4
Canada

Europe/Middle East/Africa
Thomson Learning
High Holborn House
50/51 Bedford Row
London WC1R 4LR
United Kingdom

Latin America
Thomson Learning
Seneca, 53
Colonia Polanco
11560 Mexico D.F.
Mexico

Spain/Portugal
Paraninfo
Calle/Magallanes, 25
28015 Madrid, Spain

For Eric, who nurturerd this PHD
(Poor Hopeless Daddy) in the novel and
often enigmatic world of computers

Kenneth M. Rosenberg earned his undergraduate degree at Tufts University (1963) and a Ph. D. in experimental psychology at Purdue University (1969). After graduating from Purdue, Rosenberg joined the Department of Psychology at the State University of New York/Oswego. He is the author of *Statistics for Behavioral Sciences* (Wm. C. Brown, 1990), *Stat/Tutor* (Wm. C. Brown, 1990), and co-author (with Helen Daly) of *Foundations of Behavioral Research* (Harcourt, Brace, Jovanovich, 1993).

Contents

Preface

The Excel Statistic Companion ("ESC") is a collection of demonstrations, sampling experiments, and interactive tutorials that draw on the power of Microsoft Excel for their pedagogical punch. Excel's built-in statistical functions and tools, together with its capacity to instantly update statistical output in response to new inputs, enables unlimited exploration of "What would happen if…" scenarios. Users notice immediately how markedly the spreadsheet capability for dynamic and instant change contrasts with the static and never changing information on the pages of a traditional hard-copy textbook.

As implied in the *ESC* name, I set out to develop a teaching and learning resource that would be a companion to traditional textbook coverage of descriptive and inferential statistics. In its final form, however, *ESC* is quite complete. I have used it successfully as a textbook alternative rather than as a textbook supplement in small classes ($n = 16$), but I hesitate to recommend that approach to instructors who are using the software for the first time or who teach large classes.

Even though "Excel" is in the title of the product, students will not need prior experience with Excel to have a successful experience. Running the *ESC* workbooks does require a *very limited* subset of Excel skills, and complete, detailed, and clear on-screen instructions guide all user interactions. For novice users, the *Basic Skills* tutorial and the annotated screen captures in the hard-copy *ESC User's Manual* provide an extra level of help.

A Brief History of an Idea

Although greatly enhanced by today's modern and powerful spreadsheet technology, communicating abstract statistical concepts by means of hands-on sampling experiments is not a new idea. I first encountered it as a young graduate student in 1963 when I read *Introduction to Statistical Inference* (Li, 1957). Jerome Li did not want to burden his students with sophisticated mathematical proofs. Nor did he ask his students to accept the accuracy of key statistical principles on faith. When possible (and practical) he assigned sampling experiments to foster understanding of statistical concepts.

Li constructed a normally distributed population of 500 values ($\mu = 50$, $\sigma = 10$) and wrote each individual value on a small metal-rimmed cardboard tag. Students sampled from the "tag" population as needed to demonstrate empirically many of the theoretically predicted properties of sampling distributions and the basic principles of hypothesis testing. The active learning aspect of Li's approach appealed to me, but the sampling experiments and subsequent statistical calculations were very time consuming and too impractical to do on a large scale. The bulky analog calculators of the time did little to ease the workload, and the personal computer had not yet been invented.

In the intervening years I created some computerized sampling experiments for classroom use, but those DOS-based programs quickly became obsolete with the arrival of Microsoft Windows in the early 1990s. More recently, in 2001, I was granted a sabbatical leave to create a new version of the kinds of computer-based sampling experiments, demonstrations, and opportunities for practice that had been so helpful in my earlier teaching of undergraduate statistics. With the ever-increasing availability of well-equipped PC labs on college campuses, data projectors for classroom use, and rising PC ownership in the student population, the time seemed right. The result, *The Excel Statistics Companion*, is a system for teaching statistics that is more novel and powerful than I could have imagined when I began the project.

Acknowledgements

Writing ESC in its present incarnation would not have been possible without the valuable and insightful contributions of my peer reviewers. They include Chris Chase, Claremont McKenna College, Beverly Dretzke, University of Wisconsin-Eau Claire, Chip Ettinger, Eastern Oregon University, Jon Grahe, Monmouth College, Fredrick Gravetter, SUNY College at Brockport, Steven Hall, Embry-Riddle Aeronautical University, Richard Hudiburg, University of North Alabama, Russell Hurlburt, University of Nevada, Las Vegas, Le Xuan Hy, Seattle University, Sherri Jackson, Jacksonville University, John Johnson, The Pennsylvania State University, Christopher Kello, George Mason University, William Langston, Middle Tennessee State University, G. William Lucker, University of Texas, El Paso, Mark Saviano, Brandeis University, Chris Spatz, Hendrix College, Eva Szeli, Mental Disability Rights International, Jim Zacks, Michigan State University. I am indebted to Project Manager J. Darin Derstine, who added his technical wizardry and eye for detail in the pre-production phase, Editorial Assistant Monica Sarmiento for her work on the *ESC User's Manual* and coordinating the peer review process, and my students, who endured three semesters of class testing and made many wonderful suggestions for revision. Special thanks go to my colleagues at Oswego State University of New York for supporting the sabbatical leave I needed to get ESC off the ground, Thomson Learning representative Deborah VanPatten for her personal support, and a huge thank you to Wadsworth Psychology Publisher, Vicki Knight, who gave me the encouragement and material support I needed to complete this project.

Basic Skills

Workbook: Basic Skills.xls
Worksheet: Intro

The bold outline shows the selected cell.

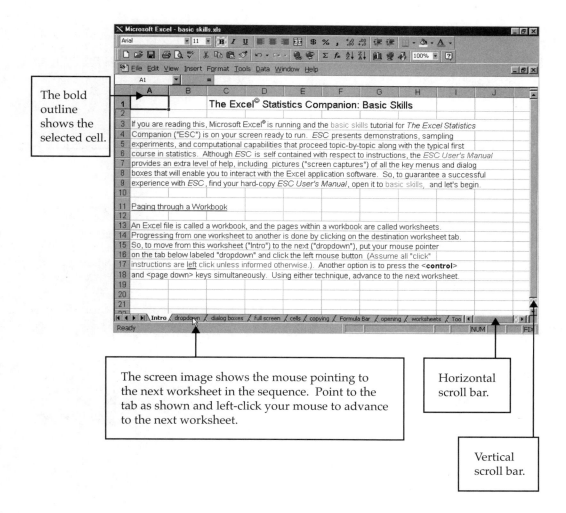

The screen image shows the mouse pointing to the next worksheet in the sequence. Point to the tab as shown and left-click your mouse to advance to the next worksheet.

Horizontal scroll bar.

Vertical scroll bar.

Workbook: Basic Skills.xls
Worksheet: dropdown

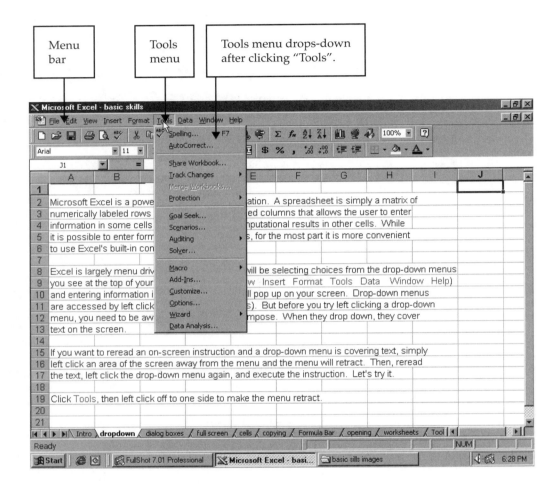

Workbook: Basic Skills.xls
Worksheet: dialog boxes

This image shows the dialog box that appears after selecting "Spelling" from theTools menu. If a spell-check box appears inviting you to change text, click the Cancel button and the "continue" box will appear as shown below. he mouse pointer is positioned on the title bar of the box.

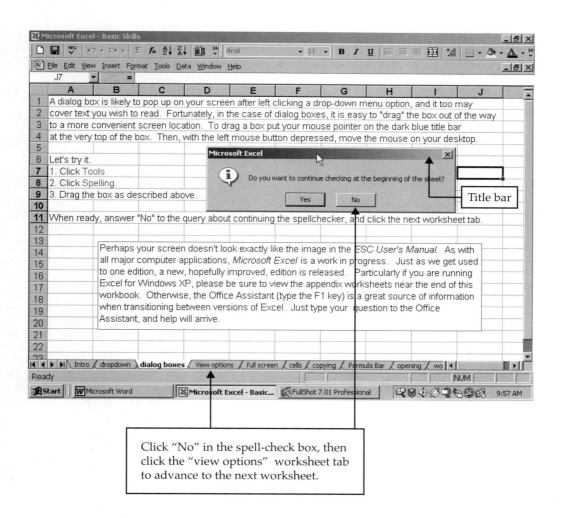

Click "No" in the spell-check box, then click the "view options" worksheet tab to advance to the next worksheet.

Workbook: Basic Skills.xls
Worksheet: full screen (a)

This image shows the "full screen" worksheet with the View drop-down menu visible. The mouse pointer is resting on the Full Screen menu choice.

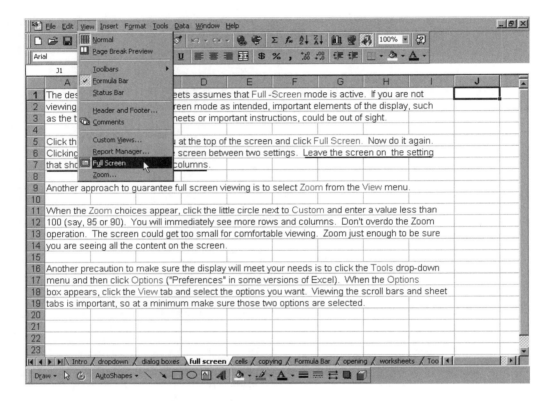

Each time you click Full Screen the view will toggle between screen settings. Leave the setting on the view that exposes the most rows and columns. Be aware, however, that the screen that exposes the most rows and columns of the Excel worksheet may also hide the maximize, minimize, and close buttons for the active window that normally appear in the upper right corner. If such a screen view is hindering your desire to minimize or close a window, click View—Full Screen again, and the buttons will come into view.

Workbook: Basic Skills.xls
Worksheet: full screen (b)

This screen shows the first step for using the zoom feature, which is to click on Zoom from the View menu.

This box shows the current Zoom setting, which is 100%

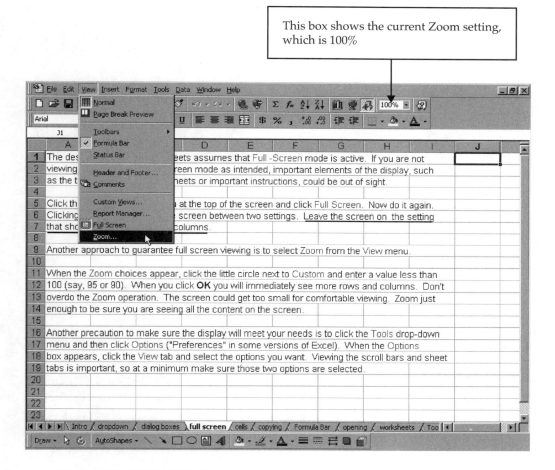

An alternative to the Full Screen command, changing the Zoom setting from 100% to a lower number such as 95%, ensures that you will see the entire screen display as intended. The screen image does, however, become smaller with each increment below 100%. So, changing the Zoom setting to less than 100% will, if taken to the extreme, make some screen elements too small for comfortable viewing.

Workbook: Basic Skills.xls
Worksheet: full screen (c)

The Zoom dialog box allows you to select an array of pre-selected screen sizes from 25% to 200%, but for our purposes it is best to enter a value in the Custom field (95% or thereabouts) as shown.

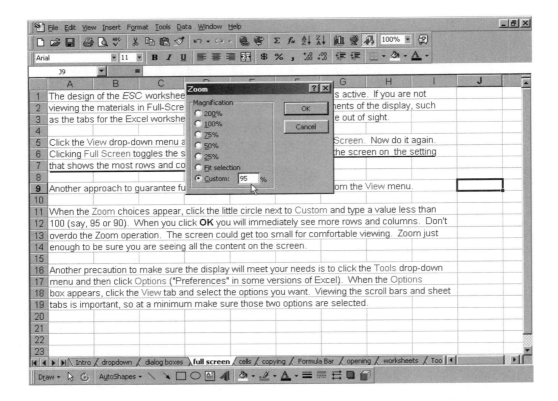

The Zoom feature contains several preset Zoom values from 25% to 200%, but you will likely have the best result entering your own value in the "custom" field.

Workbook: Basic Skills.xls
Worksheet: full screen (d)

This is the box that appears when you click Options from the Tools drop-down menu.

The mouse pointer is resting on the View tab, and the window shows the selected viewing options. Clicking other tabs (Edit, General, etc.) will give you access to other options, but they are of no concern to us at this time.

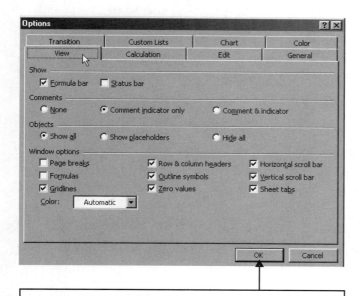

The View options you see checked here are, with the possible exception of Gridlines, important to select before running The *Excel Statistics Companion*. On a few worksheets, Gridlines is deselected. The rest of the worksheets do show the gridlines, which facilitates locating specific cells on the worksheet.

Once you have checked the View features that you wish to be incorporated into your screen display, click **OK**.

Workbook: Basic Skills.xls
Worksheet: cells

This is what your screen should look like after having selected cells A14 to A17.

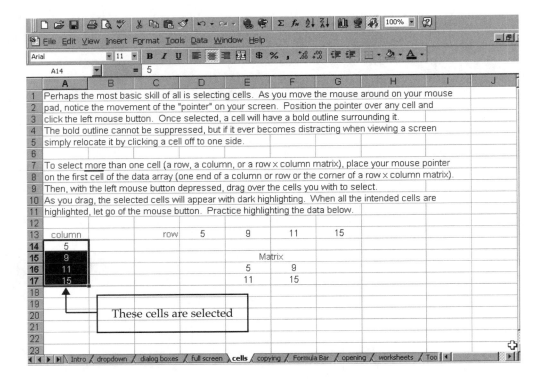

If your drag-to-highlight operation is somewhat off the mark either by including unwanted cells or failing to include intended cells, just click in any empty cell on the worksheet and the highlighting will disappear. Then try again.

Workbook: Basic Skills.xls
Worksheet: copying (a)

Once you point and click on cell H1, which contains "5," you will see a bold border surrounding the cell. This confirms that the cell is "selected." If you continue to hold the mouse pointer over the selected cell and right click, the shortcut edit menu (shown below) appears. With the mouse pointer on the Copy menu option, left click to copy the contents of cell H1.

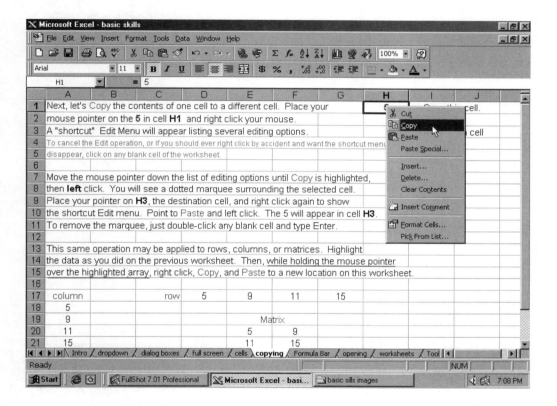

The Copy operation places the contents of the copied cells into an area of the computer's memory—a "buffer." The information will stay in the buffer until displaced by a subsequent Copy operation. The Paste command does not, therefore, empty the buffer when it pastes the copied cells. The buffer remains intact until the next "Cut" or "Copy" replaces the former contents.

Workbook: Basic Skills.xls
Worksheet: copying (b)

Now point to and click cell H3. While holding the mouse pointer over cell H3, right click and the shortcut menu will reappear. This time, click Paste from the menu, and the "5" you just copied from cell H1 will be pasted to cell H3.

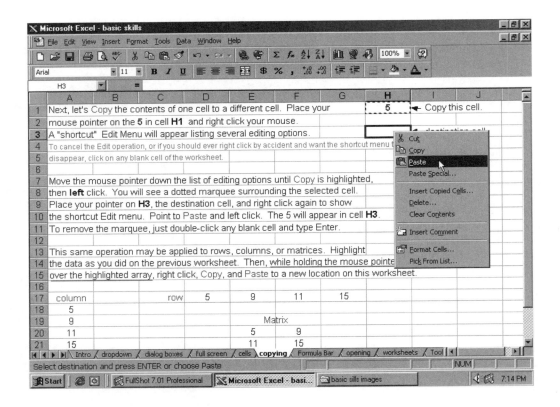

The dotted marquee will surround the selected cell as soon as the Copy command is executed. Thus, the dotted marquee shows you the specific cell (or cells) that you will be pasting when you execute the Paste command. If you make an error, a single left click in the Formula Bar will cancel the operation and rid the display of the dotted marquee. At that point you have the option of starting over.

Workbook: Basic Skills.xls
Worksheet: formula bar

In the View menu (see bottom image), clicking on Formula Bar causes a check mark to appear in the menu and the Formula Bar to be displayed on your screen. The contents of selected cells appear in the Formula bar. For example, click the yellow highlighted cell (A10) and the text that starts in cell A10 will appear in the Formula Bar. (As you see, even though "This message…" appears to extend across several cells—all the way to column D—Excel locates all the text in cell A10. That is why clicking cell A10 displays the whole sentence in the Formula Bar.)

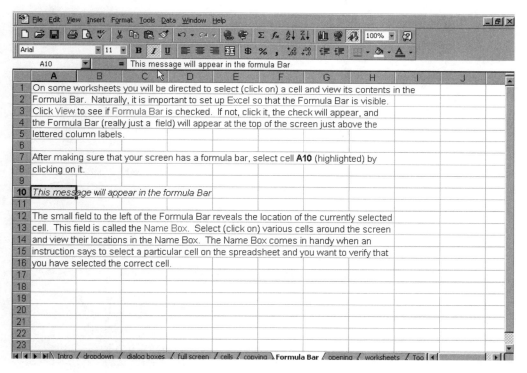

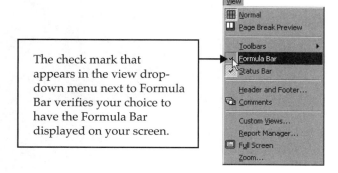

The check mark that appears in the view drop-down menu next to Formula Bar verifies your choice to have the Formula Bar displayed on your screen.

Workbook: Basic Skills.xls
Worksheet: opening (a)

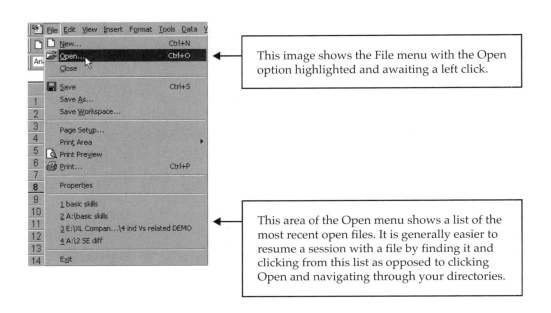

This image shows the File menu with the Open option highlighted and awaiting a left click.

This area of the Open menu shows a list of the most recent open files. It is generally easier to resume a session with a file by finding it and clicking from this list as opposed to clicking Open and navigating through your directories.

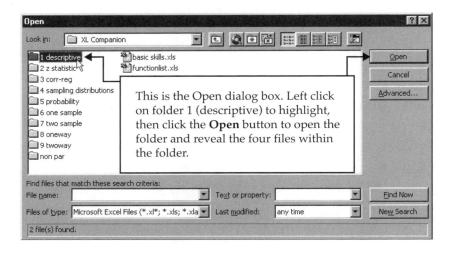

This is the Open dialog box. Left click on folder 1 (descriptive) to highlight, then click the **Open** button to open the folder and reveal the four files within the folder.

Workbook: Basic Skills
Worksheet: opening (b)

This screen shows the four Excel files in the descriptive folder with the first, "describe.xls," highlighted and ready to open with a click of the open button.

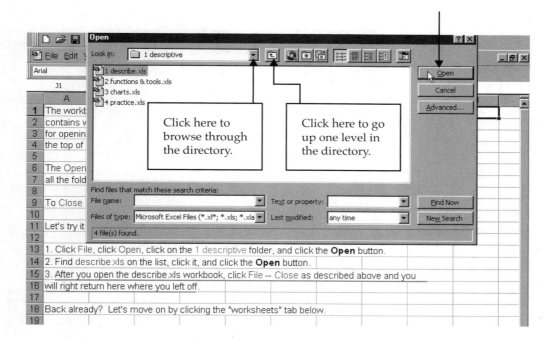

The screen image shows the mouse pointing to the next worksheet in the sequence. Point to the tab as shown and left-click your mouse to advance to the next worksheet.

Workbook: Basic Skills.xls
Worksheet: opening (c)

After opening the describe.xls file, the first worksheet in the workbook appears on the screen. You will need to click Close on the File menu (shown below) to resume your session with the basic skills workbook.

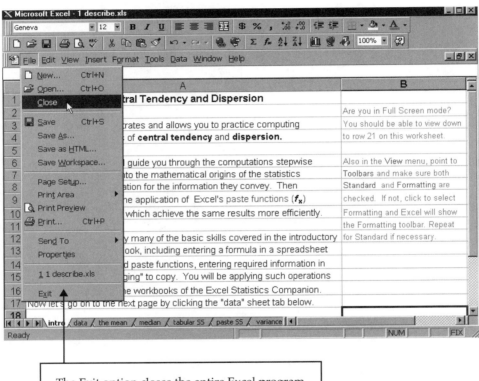

The Exit option closes the entire Excel program.
Do not click Exit unless that is your intention.
To close only the active workbook, click Close.

Workbook: Basic Skills.xls
Worksheet: worksheets

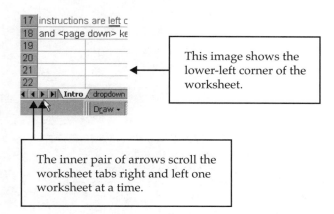

This image shows the lower-left corner of the worksheet.

The inner pair of arrows scroll the worksheet tabs right and left one worksheet at a time.

Some workbooks contain many more worksheets than will display at any one time as tabs on the bottom of the screen. To make sure that you have viewed all the worksheets in a workbook, it is a good idea to scroll the worksheet tabs to the end of the list before closing your session.

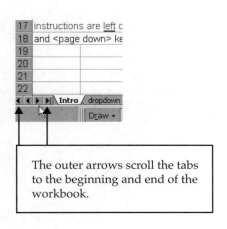

The outer arrows scroll the tabs to the beginning and end of the workbook.

Worksheet: Basic Skills.xls
Workbook: ToolPak

If the Data Analysis ToolPak is installed on your computer, you will see Data Analysis on the Tools menu. The Data Analysis menu option may appear at the bottom of the list as it does here. More current versions of Excel "learn" which functions are regularly used and put them more toward the top of the list.

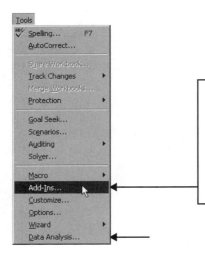

If you do not see Data Analysis listed on the Tools menu, click Add-Ins to begin the installation. Here, of course, Data Analysis does appear, so we would not have to install it. When you try to Add-In the Data Analysis ToolPak, it is possible that you may be asked to insert the CD-ROM that contains the Excel software (e.g., Microsoft Office or the Excel CD itself).

Worksheet: Basic Skills.xls
Workbook: ToolPak

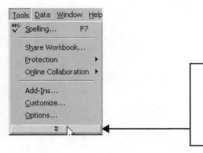

In later versions of Excel you may not immediately see all the Tools menu options. Let your pointer linger over the "more" bar and more choices will appear, including Add-Ins. A double click will produce the same result.

Check this box.

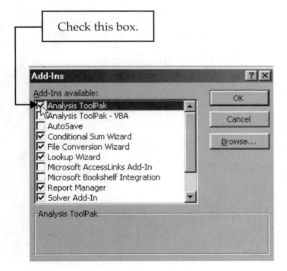

Once you click Add-Ins from the Tools menu, the last step is to click the box next to Analysis ToolPak and click OK.   In later versions of Excel, the Analysis ToolPak check box may not be first on the list of Add-Ins.

Workbook: Basic Skills.xls
Worksheet: Formula

This worksheet image shows the selection of cell J2 and the formula that
was entered in J2 (see Formula Bar). The answer (60) is displayed in the
cell. Remember, all formulas begin with an equal sign.

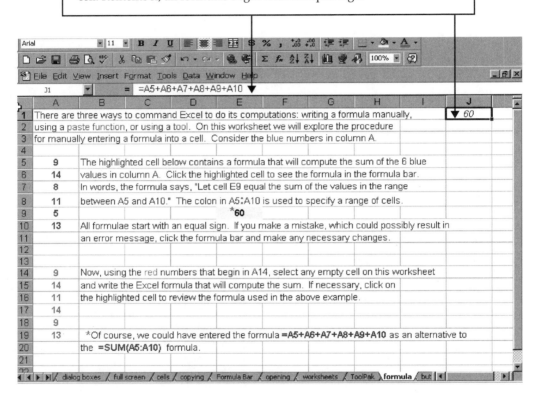

Workbook: Basic Skills.xls
Worksheet: buttons

These images show some Excel operations that may be accessed by clicking buttons on the toolbar.

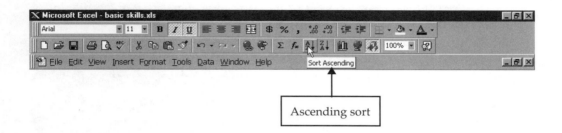

Ascending sort

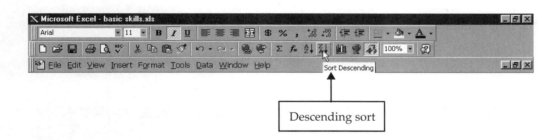

Descending sort

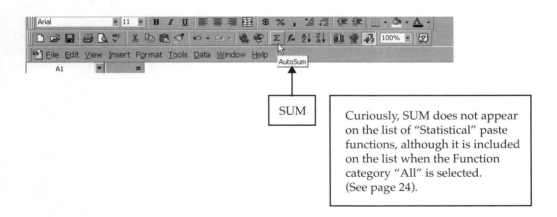

SUM

Curiously, SUM does not appear on the list of "Statistical" paste functions, although it is included on the list when the Function category "All" is selected. (See page 24).

Workbook: Basic Skills.xls
Worksheet: more buttons

If you make a procedural error and must revert back to an earlier screen state, all you have to do is click the undo button. The computer stores many previous keyboard actions, and each click of the undo button reverses those actions one at a time. If the button "grays out," it means you have reached the beginning of the operation sequence, and no further backtracking is possible.

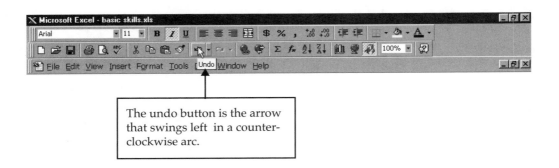

The undo button is the arrow
that swings left in a counter-
clockwise arc.

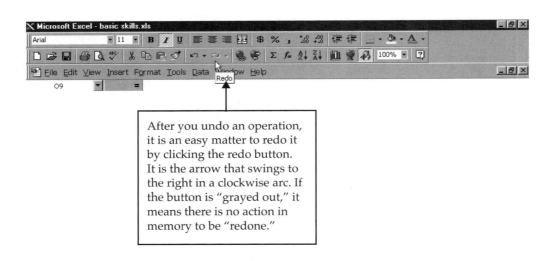

After you undo an operation,
it is an easy matter to redo it
by clicking the redo button.
It is the arrow that swings to
the right in a clockwise arc. If
the button is "grayed out," it
means there is no action in
memory to be "redone."

Workbook: Basic Skills.xls
Worksheet: functions (a,b)

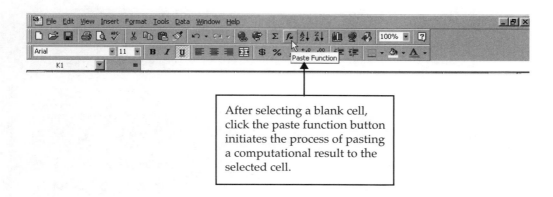

After selecting a blank cell,
click the paste function button
initiates the process of pasting
a computational result to the
selected cell.

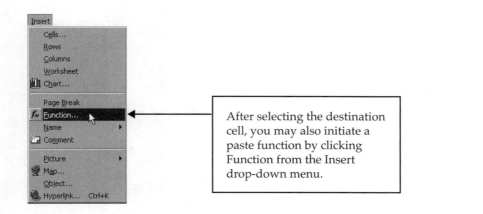

After selecting the destination
cell, you may also initiate a
paste function by clicking
Function from the Insert
drop-down menu.

Workbook: Basic Skills.xls
Worksheet: functions

There are two lists in the paste function dialog box. Click Statistics from left ("Function category") menu and a statistic (AVERAGE, in the present instance) from the right ("Function name") menu. Then click **OK**. In future sessions with Excel, use the scroll bar as needed to reveal the remaining statistical functions.

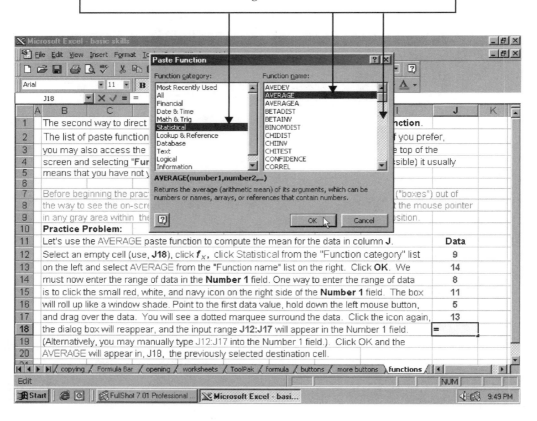

Practice Problem:
Let's use the AVERAGE paste function to compute the mean for the data in column **J**.
Select an empty cell (use, **J18**), click f_x, click Statistical from the "Function category" list
on the left and select AVERAGE from the "Function name" list on the right. Click OK. We
must now enter the range of data in the **Number 1** field. One way to enter the range of data
is to click the small red, white, and navy icon on the right side of the **Number 1** field. The box
will roll up like a window shade. Point to the first data value, hold down the left mouse button,
and drag over the data. You will see a dotted marquee surround the data. Click the icon again,
the dialog box will reappear, and the input range **J12:J17** will appear in the Number 1 field.
(Alternatively, you may manually type J12:J17 into the Number 1 field.). Click OK and the
AVERAGE will appear in, J18, the previously selected destination cell.

Data
9
14
8
11
5
13

Workbook: Basic Skills.xls
Worksheet: functions

This is the tiny spreadsheet icon that allows you to drag to select the Input Range for your data.

The last step is to fill in the dialog box for the function. In the Number 1 field, as shown, enter the range of data to which the paste function will apply—J12:J17. Click **OK** to paste the result to the selected cell (J18). Notice that the paste function result for AVERAGE appears in the box even before clicking **OK**.

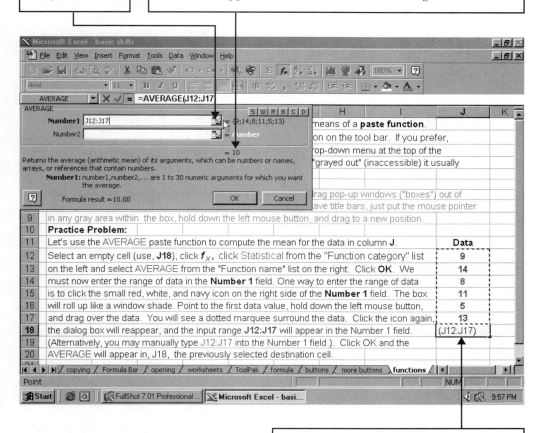

The range of numbers on which the paste function will operate will appear in the selected cell. This information also appears in the Formula Bar. If the cell is too small, not all the contents will fit in the cell, but this will not affect Excel's computation.

Workbook: Basic Skills.xls
Worksheet: error example

The "error example" worksheet shows what happens when Excel tries to put information in a cell that is too small to hold the value. The #### error message appears. One remedy is to widen the column, which also increases the width of the cells in that column. In the current example, widening the column allows the data to replace the error message in the destination cell. The procedure for widening is captured in the following images.

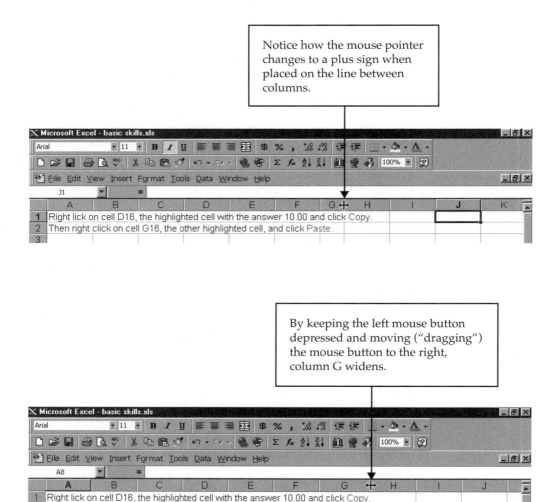

Workbook: Basic Skills.xls
Worksheet: copy & paste special

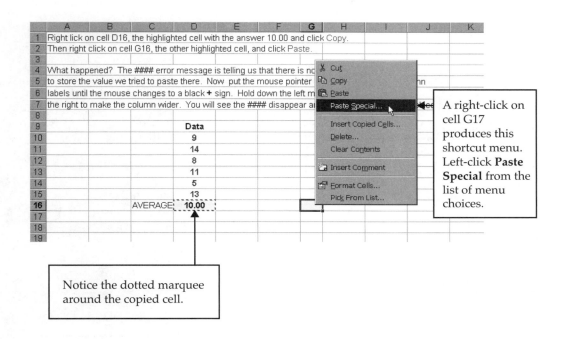

	A	B	C	D	E	F	G	H	I	J	K
1	Right lick on cell D16, the highlighted cell with the answer 10.00 and click Copy.										
2	Then right click on cell G16, the other highlighted cell, and click Paste.										
3											
4	What happened? The #### error message is telling us that there is no										
5	to store the value we tried to paste there. Now put the mouse pointer									hn		
6	labels until the mouse changes to a black + sign. Hold down the left m										
7	the right to make the column wider. You will see the #### disappear a										
8											
9				**Data**							
10				9							
11				14							
12				8							
13				11							
14				5							
15				13							
16			AVERAGE	10.00							
17											
18											
19											

Shortcut menu:
- ✄ Cut
- Copy
- Paste
- Paste Special...
- Insert Copied Cells...
- Delete...
- Clear Contents
- Insert Comment
- Format Cells...
- Pick From List...

A right-click on cell G17 produces this shortcut menu. Left-click **Paste Special** from the list of menu choices.

Notice the dotted marquee around the copied cell.

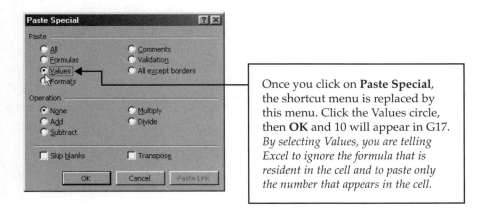

Paste Special

Paste
- All
- Formulas
- Values
- Formats
- Comments
- Validation
- All except borders

Operation
- None
- Add
- Subtract
- Multiply
- Divide

- Skip blanks
- Transpose

OK   Cancel   Paste Link

Once you click on **Paste Special**, the shortcut menu is replaced by this menu. Click the Values circle, then **OK** and 10 will appear in G17. *By selecting Values, you are telling Excel to ignore the formula that is resident in the cell and to paste only the number that appears in the cell.*

Workbook: Basic Skills.xls
Worksheet: drag to copy

	Data A	Data B	
	9	17	
	14	18	
	8	14	
	11	19	
	5	12	
	13	16	
AVERAGE	**10.00**		

Cell D17 holds an AVERAGE. The formula may be dragged to cell E17 and thereby produce an AVERAGE for Data B. The key is positioning the mouse on the lower right of the cell until the pointer changes to the plus sign. Once you see the plus sign, hold down the left mouse button, drag one cell to the right, and release the mouse button.

	Data A	Data B	
	9	17	
	14	18	
	8	14	
	11	19	
	5	12	
	13	16	
AVERAGE	**10.00**		

This is what the display will look like after the drag operation—but before you release the left mouse button.

	Data A	Data B	
	9	17	
	14	18	
	8	14	
	11	19	
	5	12	
	13	16	
AVERAGE	10.00	16.00	

When you release the left mouse button the AVERAGE of Data set B will appear in cell E17. Excel "knows" that you want the AVERAGE of the Data B column even though you dragged the formula **AVERAGE(D11:D16)** from column A. This is called "indexing." You will see the formula **AVERAGE(E11:E16)** in the Formula Bar when cell E17 is selected.

Workbook: Basic Skills.xls
Worksheet: tools

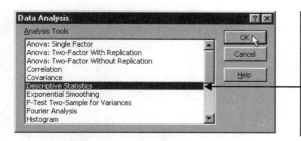

This box pops up when you click **Data Analysis** from the **Tools** drop-down menu. The instruction on the worksheet asks for you to click **Descriptive Statistics** from the list of tools.

You do not need to type the $ signs when entering ranges. Excel adds them automatically.

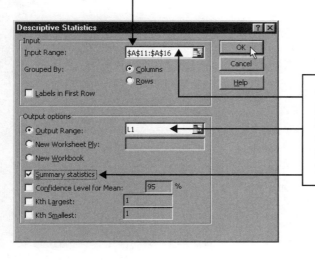

This image shows the Descriptive Statistics dialog box as it should look after following the on-screen instructions. Click **OK** once you have made these entries.

Workbook: Basic Skills.xls
Worksheet: col. Width

Widening columns is sometimes necessary to have a proper view of an output table.

When the pointer changes to a plus sign, drag to widen the column.

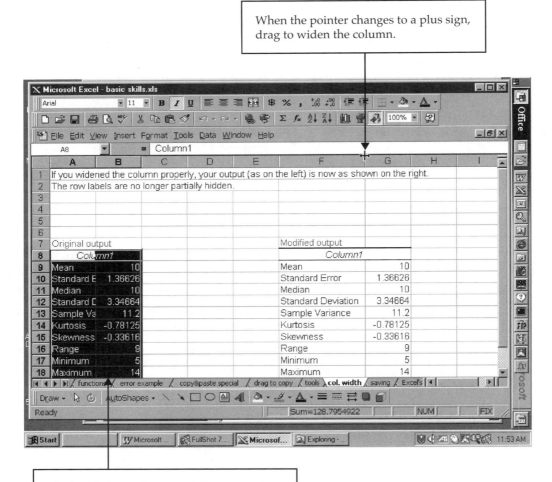

The highlighting that is initially present in the output table of a Data Analysis Tool may be turned off by clicking in any empty cell of the worksheet.

Workbook: Basic Skills.xls
Worksheet: saving

If you wish to save any work you have completed in an Excel workbook, save it using the **Save As** option from the **File** menu. You will, of course, need to tell Excel where to save the file (the "Save in" field) and enter a file name (the File name field).

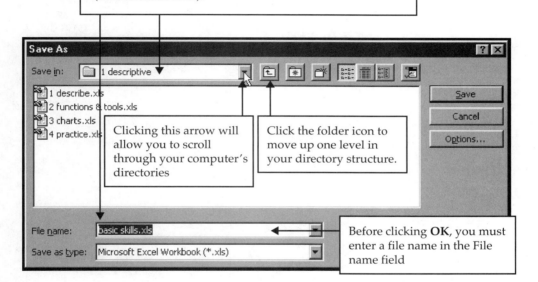

Save As   ? X

Save in: [📁] 1 descriptive ▼

1 describe.xls
2 functions & tools.xls
3 charts.xls
4 practice.xls

Save
Cancel
Options...

Clicking this arrow will allow you to scroll through your computer's directories

Click the folder icon to move up one level in your directory structure.

File name: basic skills.xls

Save as type: Microsoft Excel Workbook (*.xls)

Before clicking **OK**, you must enter a file name in the File name field

The CD-ROM that contains your Excel software cannot be modified with a save operation. Using **Save As** from the File menu, save a file on which you are working to your hard drive, floppy, zip disk,—or another CD-ROM if you have the hardware on your computer. A good aspect of this minor inconvenience is that it is impossible to corrupt a file unintentionally. You will always have the same unchanged pristine version of the software you purchased.

Workbook: Basic Skills.xls
Worksheet: Excel help

The paste function dialog box has two question marks that you may click to access help.

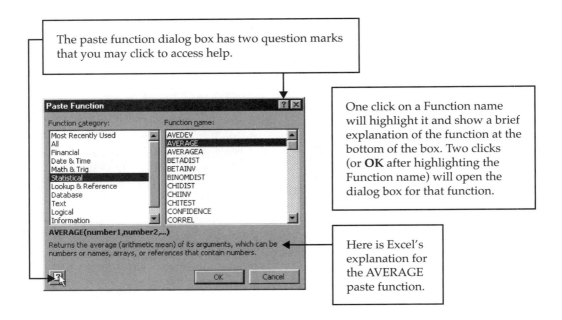

One click on a Function name will highlight it and show a brief explanation of the function at the bottom of the box. Two clicks (or **OK** after highlighting the Function name) will open the dialog box for that function.

Here is Excel's explanation for the AVERAGE paste function.

When using a Data Analysis Tool, the question mark for help is here.

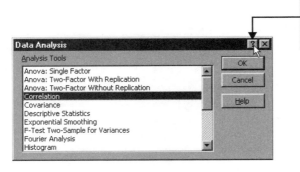

Workbook: Basic Skills.xls
Worksheet: Excel help

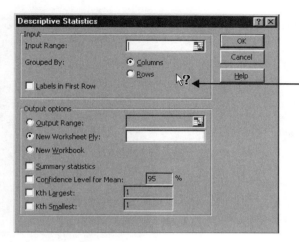

After clicking the question mark button, the question mark becomes bold and moves along with the mouse pointer. The next step is to left-click. A box will pop up with a general description of the tool along with a link to specific instructions that relate to each query in the dialog box.

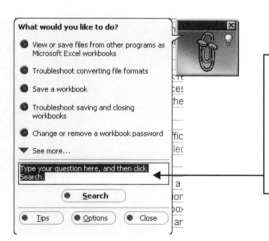

This is Excel's office assistant, which is accessed by clicking the question mark at the top right of your screen or the Help menu on the menu bar. Your assistant might look a little different than mine. Type in your question where shown and Excel will do its best to help.

Describing Data

Folder: 01 Descriptive Statistics
Workbook: Describing Data.xls
Worksheet: data

To highlight ("select") the random values, hold down the left mouse button and drag from row 3 to row 13.

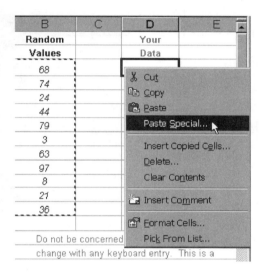

With your mouse pointer on cell D3, right click and click **Paste Special** on the shortcut menu.

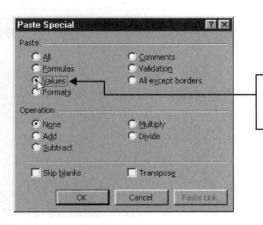

In the paste special dialog box be sure to click the Values circle before clicking **OK**.

Folder 01: Descriptive Statistics
Workbook: Describing Data.xls
Worksheet: the mean

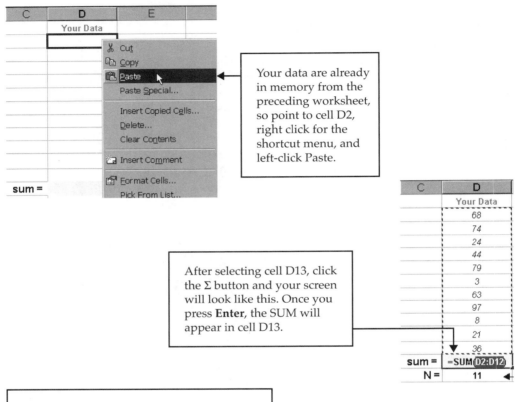

Your data are already in memory from the preceding worksheet, so point to cell D2, right click for the shortcut menu, and left-click Paste.

After selecting cell D13, click the Σ button and your screen will look like this. Once you press **Enter**, the SUM will appear in cell D13.

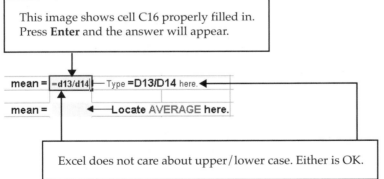

This image shows cell C16 properly filled in. Press **Enter** and the answer will appear.

mean = =d13/d14 ──Type **=D13/D14** here.◄

mean = ◄──Locate AVERAGE here.

Excel does not care about upper/lower case. Either is OK.

Folder 01: Descriptive Statistics
Workbook: Describing Data.xls
Worksheet: the mean

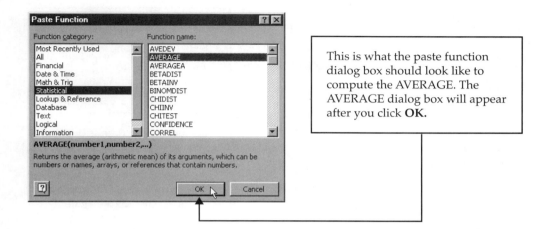

This is what the paste function dialog box should look like to compute the AVERAGE. The AVERAGE dialog box will appear after you click **OK.**

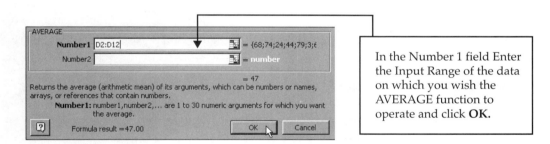

In the Number 1 field Enter the Input Range of the data on which you wish the AVERAGE function to operate and click **OK.**

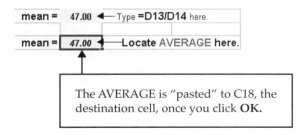

The AVERAGE is "pasted" to C18, the destination cell, once you click **OK.**

Folder: 01 Descriptive Statistics
Workbook: Describing Data.xls
Worksheet: median

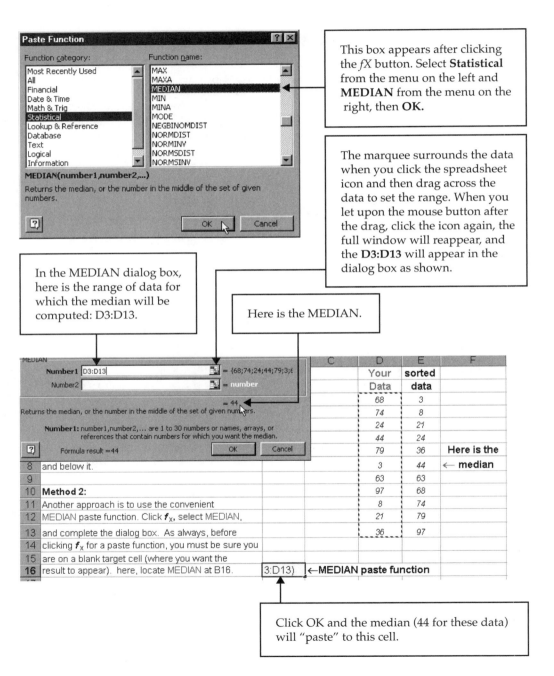

This box appears after clicking the *fX* button. Select **Statistical** from the menu on the left and **MEDIAN** from the menu on the right, then **OK**.

The marquee surrounds the data when you click the spreadsheet icon and then drag across the data to set the range. When you let upon the mouse button after the drag, click the icon again, the full window will reappear, and the **D3:D13** will appear in the dialog box as shown.

In the MEDIAN dialog box, here is the range of data for which the median will be computed: D3:D13.

Here is the MEDIAN.

Click OK and the median (44 for these data) will "paste" to this cell.

Folder: 01: Descriptive Statistics
Workbook: Describing Data.xls
Worksheet: tabular SS

Keep in mind that these are randomly selected values. They will undoubtedly produce answers different from the ones on your screen.

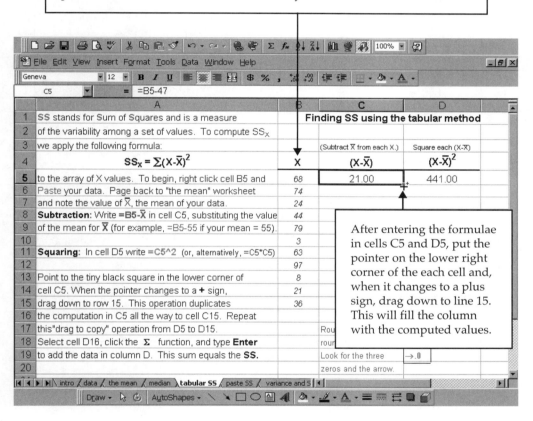

	A	B	C	D
			Finding SS using the tabular method	
1	SS stands for Sum of Squares and is a measure			
2	of the variability among a set of values. To compute SS_X			
3	we apply the following formula:		(Subtract $\overline{X}$ from each X.)	Square each (X-$\overline{X}$)
4	$SS_X = \Sigma(X-\overline{X})^2$	X	$(X-\overline{X})$	$(X-\overline{X})^2$
5	to the array of X values. To begin, right click cell B5 and	68	21.00	441.00
6	Paste your data. Page back to "the mean" worksheet	74		
7	and note the value of $\overline{X}$, the mean of your data.	24		
8	**Subtraction:** Write =B5-$\overline{X}$ in cell C5, substituting the value	44		
9	of the mean for $\overline{X}$ (for example, =B5-55 if your mean = 55).	79		
10		3		
11	**Squaring:** In cell D5 write =C5^2 (or, alternatively, =C5*C5)	63		
12		97		
13	Point to the tiny black square in the lower corner of	8		
14	cell C5. When the pointer changes to a **+** sign,	21		
15	drag down to row 15. This operation duplicates	36		
16	the computation in C5 all the way to cell C15. Repeat			
17	this "drag to copy" operation from D5 to D15.		Rou	
18	Select cell D16, click the **Σ** function, and type **Enter**		roun	
19	to add the data in column D. This sum equals the **SS.**		Look for the three	→.0
20			zeros and the arrow.	

The formula bar shows: C5 = =B5-47

After entering the formulae in cells C5 and D5, put the pointer on the lower right corner of the each cell and, when it changes to a plus sign, drag down to line 15. This will fill the column with the computed values.

Finding SS using the tabular method

X	(Subtract X̄ from each X.) $(X-\bar{X})$	Square each (X-X̄) $(X-\bar{X})^2$
68	21.00	441.00
74	27.00	729.00
24	-23.00	529.00
44	-3.00	9.00
79	32.00	1024.00
3	-44.00	1936.00
63	16.00	256.00
97	50.00	2500.00
8	-39.00	1521.00
21	-26.00	676.00
36	-11.00	121.00
	SS =	9742.00

This image shows the table filled in following the drag operation. The drag operation copies the formula to the other cells. The highlighted cell shows the SUM (Σ button) for the data above. Your answer will be different because your data will be different.

Raw data.

Notice how the Excel formulae and the capacity to drag them here and there enable us to follow hand calculation methods with a minimum of work. The advantage to viewing the hand calculation methods is that they convey substantial information about the statistic. Here, for example, it is easy to see that the Sum of Squares statistic is the sum of the squared deviations of each data value from the mean of all the data values. If we used the easier DEVSQ function to get this answer in one step, the latter aspect of the SS statistic would not be as obvious.

Folder: 01: Descriptive Statistics
Workbook: Describing data.xls
Worksheet: paste SS

The syntax for the DEVSQ paste function appears in Formula Bar.

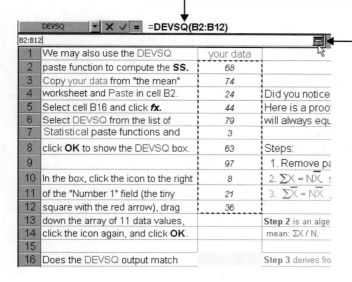

Notice how the window rolls up like a window shade when dragging to set the range for the data. The dotted marquee shows the result of the drag operation. Click the icon again and the full window will reappear with the range B2:B12 in the "Number 1" field.

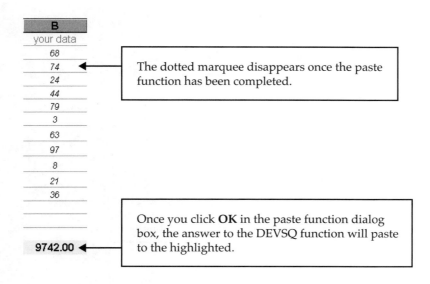

The dotted marquee disappears once the paste function has been completed.

Once you click **OK** in the paste function dialog box, the answer to the DEVSQ function will paste to the highlighted.

Folder: 01 Descriptive Statistics
Workbook: Describing Data.xls
Worksheet: variance and SD

After you type a formula
into cells B8 and B9, press
the **Enter** key and the
solution to each formula
will appear.

These are the SS and N values for the data in column E.
Your data and statistics will have different values.

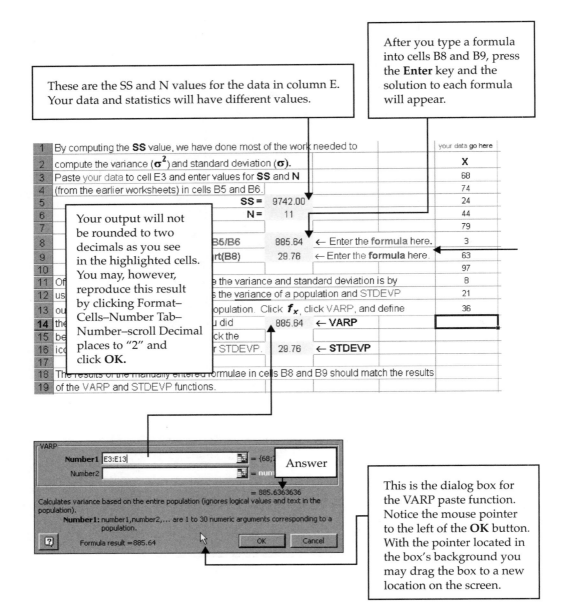

1	By computing the **SS** value, we have done most of the work needed to			your data **go here**
2	compute the variance (σ^2) and standard deviation (σ).			X
3	Paste your data to cell E3 and enter values for **SS** and N			68
4	(from the earlier worksheets) in cells B5 and B6.			74
5		SS =	9742.00	24
6		N =	11	44
7				79
8	B5/B6	885.64	← Enter the **formula** here.	3
9	rt(B8)	29.76	← Enter the **formula** here.	63
10				97
11	the variance and standard deviation is by		8
12	the variance of a population and STDEVP		21
13	opulation. Click f_x, click VARP, and define		36
14	u did	885.64	← **VARP**	
15	ck the			
16	r STDEVP.	29.76	← **STDEVP**	
17				
18	formulae in cells B8 and B9 should match the results			
19	of the VARP and STDEVP functions.			

Your output will not
be rounded to two
decimals as you see
in the highlighted cells.
You may, however,
reproduce this result
by clicking Format–
Cells–Number Tab–
Number–scroll Decimal
places to "2" and
click **OK.**

VARP
Number1 E3:E13   = {68;
Number2   = num

Answer

= 885.6363636
Calculates variance based on the entire population (ignores logical values and text in the
population).
Number1: number1,number2,... are 1 to 30 numeric arguments corresponding to a
population.

Formula result =885.64   OK   Cancel

This is the dialog box for
the VARP paste function.
Notice the mouse pointer
to the left of the **OK** button.
With the pointer located in
the box's background you
may drag the box to a new
location on the screen.

Folder: 01 Descriptive Statistics
Workbook: Describing Data.xls
Worksheet: variance and SD

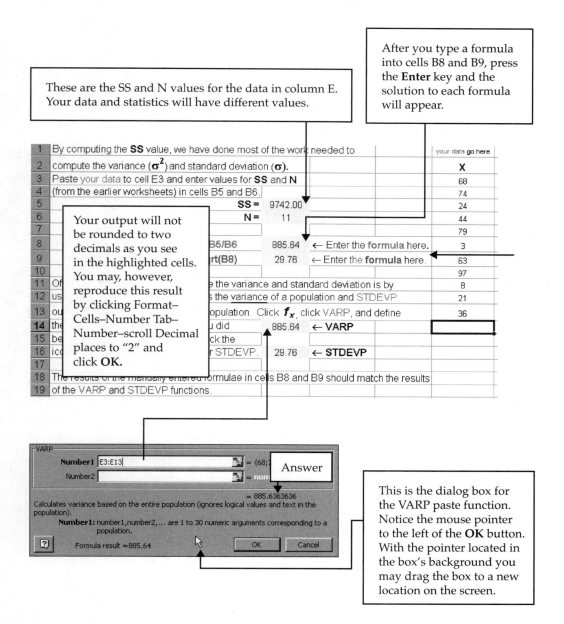

These are the SS and N values for the data in column E.
Your data and statistics will have different values.

After you type a formula
into cells B8 and B9, press
the **Enter** key and the
solution to each formula
will appear.

1	By computing the **SS** value, we have done most of the work needed to				your data go here
2	compute the variance (σ^2) and standard deviation (σ).				X
3	Paste your data to cell E3 and enter values for **SS** and N				68
4	(from the earlier worksheets) in cells B5 and B6.				74
5		SS =	9742.00		24
6		N =	11		44
7					79
8	B5/B6		885.64	← Enter the **formula** here.	3
9	rt(B8)		29.76	← Enter the **formula** here.	63
10					97
11	the variance and standard deviation is by				8
12	the variance of a population and STDEVP				21
13	opulation. Click f_x, click VARP, and define				36
14	u did	885.64	← VARP		
15	ck the				
16	r STDEVP.	29.76	← STDEVP		
17					
18	The results of the manually entered formulae in cells B8 and B9 should match the results				
19	of the VARP and STDEVP functions.				

Your output will not
be rounded to two
decimals as you see
in the highlighted cells.
You may, however,
reproduce this result
by clicking Format–
Cells–Number Tab–
Number–scroll Decimal
places to "2" and
click **OK.**

VARP

Number1 E3:E13   = {68;
Number2   = num

                                         = 885.6363636
Calculates variance based on the entire population (ignores logical values and text in the
population).
    Number1: number1,number2,... are 1 to 30 numeric arguments corresponding to a
            population.

[?]   Formula result =885.64   OK   Cancel

Answer

This is the dialog box for
the VARP paste function.
Notice the mouse pointer
to the left of the **OK** button.
With the pointer located in
the box's background you
may drag the box to a new
location on the screen.

CHAPTER 1-2

Functions and Tools

Folder: 01 Descriptive Statistics
Workbook: Functions and Tools.xls
Worksheet: rank and percentile

Once you click Data Analysis on the Tools menu, scroll this list to find the Rank and Percentile Tool, then Click **OK.**

The Rank and Percentile dialog box appears after you click the sequence **Tools–Data Analysis–Rank and Percentile.**

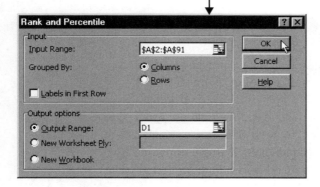

This is what the Rank and Percentile dialog box should look like once you have entered the required information. Excel automatically includes the $ signs in the syntax if you use the drag technique to set the Input Range. You do *not* need to type the $ signs if you are typing in the information manually. The last step is to click **OK.**

The Rank and Percentile output table will initially appear highlighted on the spreadsheet. Click on any empty cell to remove highlighting.

Folder: 01 Descriptive Statistics
Workbook: Functions and Tools.xls
Worksheet: pasteEX

Here you see the *fx* button ready to be clicked.

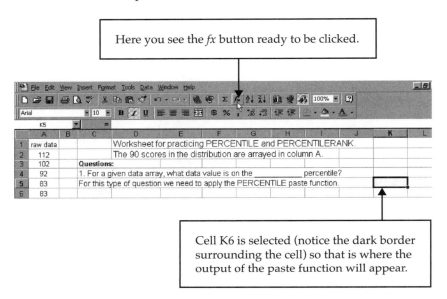

Cell K6 is selected (notice the dark border surrounding the cell) so that is where the output of the paste function will appear.

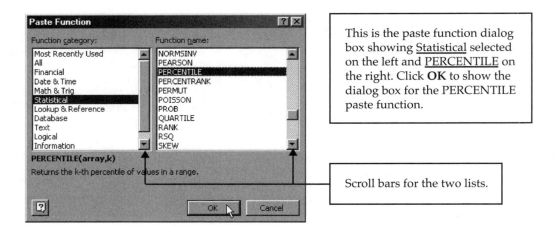

This is the paste function dialog box showing <u>Statistical</u> selected on the left and <u>PERCENTILE</u> on the right. Click **OK** to show the dialog box for the PERCENTILE paste function.

Scroll bars for the two lists.

Folder: 01 Descriptive Statistics
Workbook: Functions and Tools
Worksheet: pasteEX

Be sure to include a decimal to enter
the percentile as a proportion.

Here is the PERCENTILE
dialog box properly filled
in. A click on **OK** "pastes"
the answer in the
destination cell.

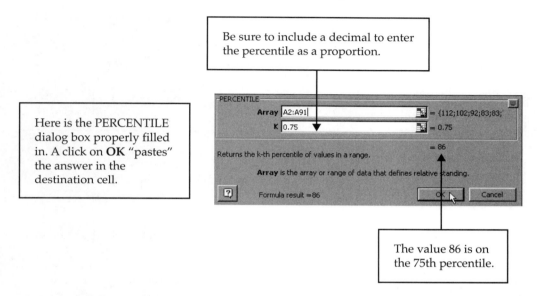

The value 86 is on
the 75th percentile.

The reverse process, finding a percentile given a data value, is shown below using the
PERCENTRANK paste function.

This tells Excel that the data
range is cell A2 to cell A91.

X is a value in the
array for which we
want the percentile.
The function reports
that 65 is on the 42.6
percentile.

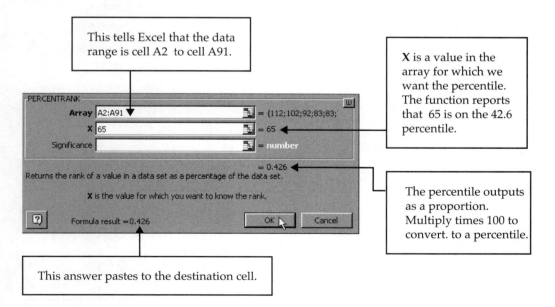

The percentile outputs
as a proportion.
Multiply times 100 to
convert. to a percentile.

This answer pastes to the destination cell.

Folder: 01 Descriptive Statistics
Workbook: Functions and Tools.xls
Worksheet: descriptive

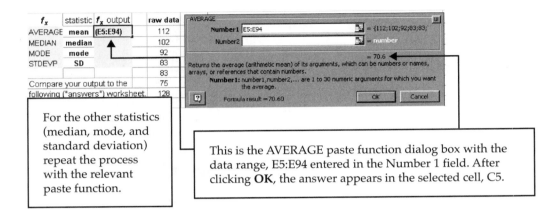

For the other statistics (median, mode, and standard deviation) repeat the process with the relevant paste function.

This is the AVERAGE paste function dialog box with the data range, E5:E94 entered in the Number 1 field. After clicking **OK**, the answer appears in the selected cell, C5.

After using paste functions to compute values for the statistics on the left, the worksheet introduces an alternative method: the Descriptive Statistics tool.

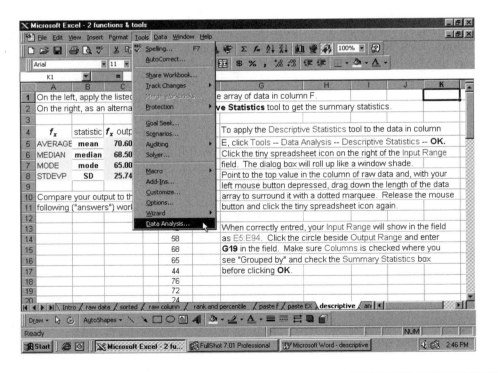

Folder: 01 Descriptive Statistics
Workbook: Functions and Tools
Worksheet: descriptive

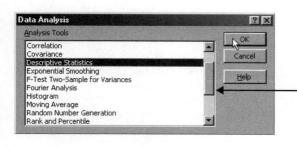

Scroll the Analysis Tools to find Descriptive Statistics, and click **OK**.

The Input Range tells Excel where to find the data. Here, the data are in the range of cells E5 to E94. The dollar signs, which you may notice appearing from time to time in various boxes, may be ignored. Just enter E5:E94 or e5:e94 and Excel takes it from there.

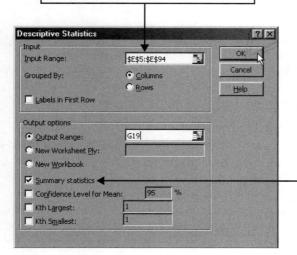

This is what the Descriptive Statistics dialog box should look like before you click **OK**.

Select Summary Statistics.

B	C	D
	Finding SS using the tabular method	
	(Subtract X̄ from each X.)	Square each (X-X̄)
X	**(X-X̄)**	**(X-X̄)^2**
68	21.00	441.00
74	27.00	729.00
24	-23.00	529.00
44	-3.00	9.00
79	32.00	1024.00
3	-44.00	1936.00
63	16.00	256.00
97	50.00	2500.00
8	-39.00	1521.00
21	-26.00	676.00
36	-11.00	121.00
	SS =	**9742.00**

This image shows the table filled in following the drag operation. The drag operation copies the formula to the other cells. The highlighted cell shows the SUM (Σ button) for the data above. Your answer will be different because your data will be different.

Raw data.

Notice how the Excel formulae and the capacity to drag them here and there enable us to follow hand calculation methods with a minimum of work. The advantage to viewing the hand calculation methods is that they convey substantial information about the statistic. Here, for example, it is easy to see that the Sum of Squares statistic is the sum of the squared deviations of each data value from the mean of all the data values. If we used the easier DEVSQ function to get this answer in one step, the latter aspect of the SS statistic would not be as obvious.

Folder 01: Descriptive Statistics
Workbook: Functions and Tools.xls
Worksheet: descriptive

Initially, Excel displays the output table with highlighting.

In practice, it is likely you will have to widen the destination column to read the statistic labels. Here, for your convenience, column G has already been widened to allow the table to display properly.

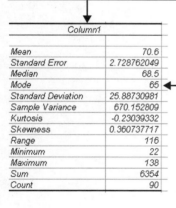

Clicking anywhere in the worksheet causes the highlighting to disappear so the table looks like this.

Check to see how closely these values match the values computed by the paste functions.

Frequency Distributions

Folder: 01 Descriptive Statistics
Workbook: Frequency Distributions.xls
Worksheet: make ungrouped

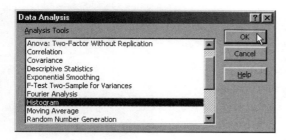

After clicking Data Analysis on the Tools drop-down menu, scroll the list of Tools to Histogram, click it to highlight, then click **OK.**

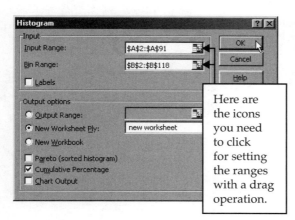

Here are the icons you need to click for setting the ranges with a drag operation.

If you enter the Input Range and Bin ranges manually, you will not need to type the $ signs. Excel adds $$ when you set ranges using the drag method, which is to click the icon, drag the dotted marquee over the range, and click the icon again. Recall that the box will roll up like a window shade when you first click the icon. You may have to look around the screen a bit to spot the icon for the final click.

Folder: 01 Descriptive Statistics
Workbook: Frequency Distributions.xls
Worksheets: make grouped / edit table

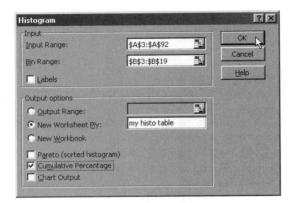

Enter the information in the fields
as shown and click **OK**. The
Histogram tool will then output a
grouped frequency distribution.

original **unedited** Histogram output table

Bin	Frequency	Cumulative %
28	4	4.44%
35	5	10.00%
42	3	13.33%
49	7	21.11%
56	9	31.11%
63	9	41.11%
70	9	51.11%
77	11	63.33%
84	8	72.22%
91	6	78.89%
98	6	85.56%
105	3	88.89%
112	4	93.33%
119	2	95.56%
126	1	96.67%
133	2	98.89%
140	1	100.00%
More	0	100.00%

When you drag to highlight the table
in preparation for the descending sort,
be careful to leave off the "More" row.

Making Charts

Folder: 01 Descriptive Statistics
Workbook: Making Charts.xls
Worksheet: make chart

Your screen will look like this after you click the chart wizard button. Select "Column" as your chart type then click "Next".

Chart Wizard button.

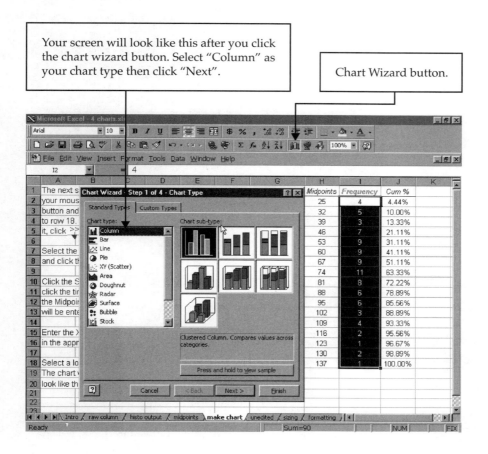

Folder: 01 Descriptive Statistics
Workbook: Making Charts.xls
Worksheet: make chart

Clicking "Next" on the step 1 dialog box brings up this box. Click on the Series tab and the screen shown below will come into view.

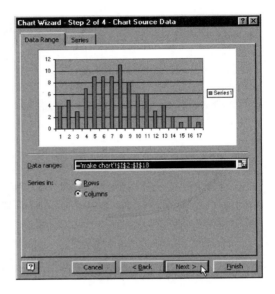

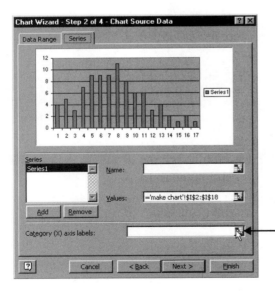

If you wish, click the Name field and enter a name for the dependent variable ("Series"). Enter Category X axis labels (the bottom field in the window) by clicking the spreadsheet icon at the right side of the field, drag across the array of edited Bin values ("Midpoints"), click the icon again, and click the Next button to finish. The proper scale for the X axis will replace the original "1, 2, 3, . . ."

Folder: 01 Descriptive Statistics
Workbook: Making Charts.xls
Worksheet: make chart

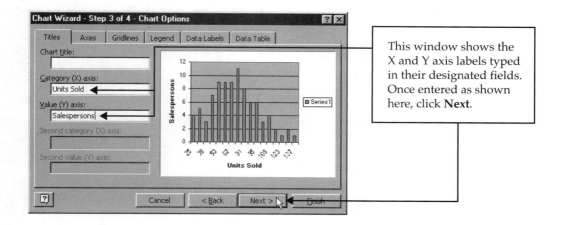

This window shows the X and Y axis labels typed in their designated fields. Once entered as shown here, click **Next**.

It is a matter of choice where you want the chart to appear—either on a new worksheet or on the resident "make chart" worksheet (select "As object in"). Editing seems to go more smoothly with the latter choice. You may always copy and paste the chart to its own worksheet later or just drag the chart to a blank area of the current worksheet. To print the chart, select it with a click inside its border (you will see the "handles" appear), and click File–Print.

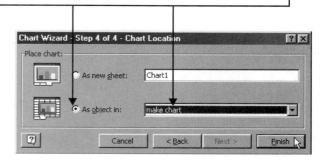

Folder: 01 Descriptive Statistics
Workbook: Making Charts.xls
Worksheet: unedited

This is what your Excel screen will look like if you
select the "as object in" option to display your chart.
The next step is to edit the crude chart to incorporate
your appearance demands.

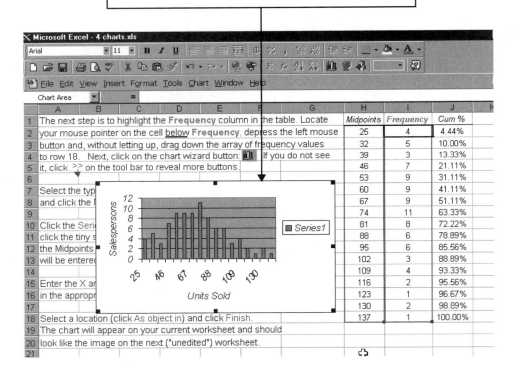

Folder: 01 Descriptive Statistics
Workbook: Making Charts.xls
Worksheet: formatting

Right-click the legend box to clear or to access the
Format menu that pertains to the Legend.

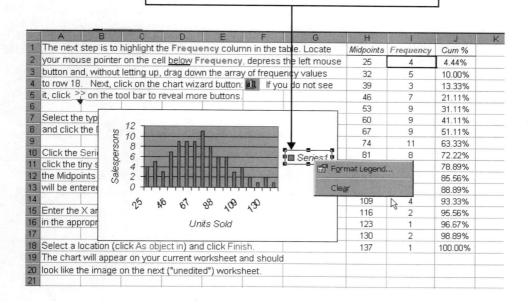

	A	B	C	D	E	F	G	H	I	J	K
1	The next step is to highlight the **Frequency** column in the table. Locate							*Midpoints*	*Frequency*	*Cum %*	
2	your mouse pointer on the cell below **Frequency**, depress the left mouse							25	4	4.44%	
3	button and, without letting up, drag down the array of frequency values							32	5	10.00%	
4	to row 18. Next, click on the chart wizard button: ▥ If you do not see							39	3	13.33%	
5	it, click >> on the tool bar to reveal more buttons.							46	7	21.11%	
6								53	9	31.11%	
7	Select the typ							60	9	41.11%	
8	and click the							67	9	51.11%	
9								74	11	63.33%	
10	Click the Seri							81	8	72.22%	
11	click the tiny s									78.89%	
12	the Midpoints									85.56%	
13	will be entere									88.89%	
14								109	4	93.33%	
15	Enter the X a							116	2	95.56%	
16	in the appropr							123	1	96.67%	
17								130	2	98.89%	
18	Select a location (click As object in) and click Finish.							137	1	100.00%	
19	The chart will appear on your current worksheet and should										
20	look like the image on the next ("unedited") worksheet.										
21											

Folder: 01Descriptive Statistics
Workbook: Making Charts.xls
Worksheet: formatting

Point to the background of the chart and right click for the shortcut menu.
Left-click Clear to remove the gray background.

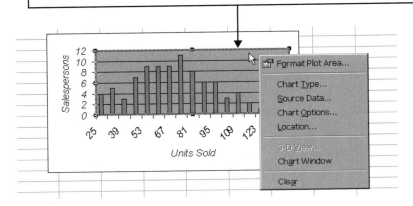

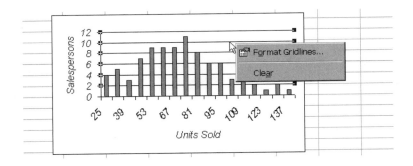

Use the same
shortcut menu
to clear the grid
lines.

Folder: 01 Descriptive Statistics
Workbook: Making Charts.xls
Worksheet: sizing

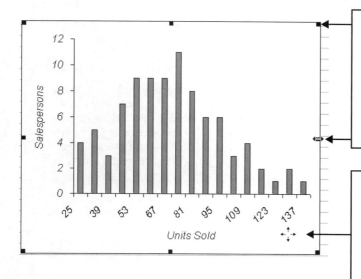

Click slightly within the chart border to expose the tiny square "handles." Then, position the mouse pointer on a handle until the pointer changes to a double pointed arrow ⇔ and drag to resize.

Holding a left click within the chart border changes the mouse pointer to an ornate plus sign and permits dragging the whole chart around the screen.

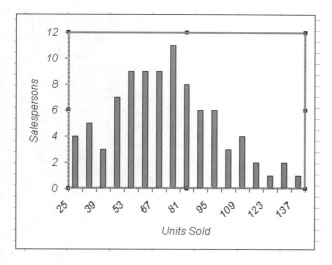

You may select the inner portion of the chart and apply the same drag operation, but resizing the inner portion is limited by the dimension of the outer portion.

Folder: 01Descriptive Statistics
Workbook: Making Charts.xls
Worksheet: formatting

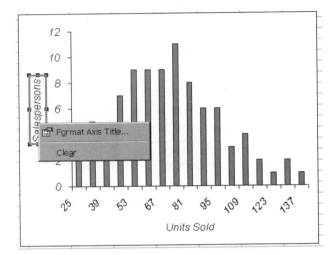

Point to any element of the chart (here, illustrated with an axis label), right click for the shortcut menu, and left click **Format** to access the relevant formatting option.

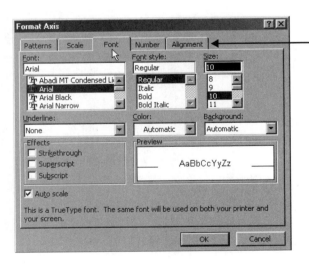

Each tab in the Format menu reveals a different formatting option. This image is the Font menu, which will enable you to control the size of the type used for the axis label selected in the above chart image.

Folder: 01 Descriptive Statistics
Workbook: Making Charts.xls
Worksheet: formatting

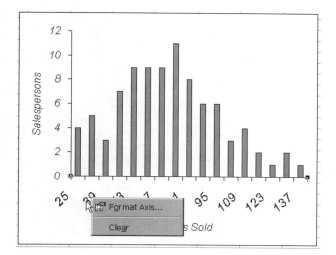

If Excel displays your chart with print that is too large, just point to the axis value (as shown here), right click, and left click Format axis. The Format menu will appear as above, and you may enter your change.

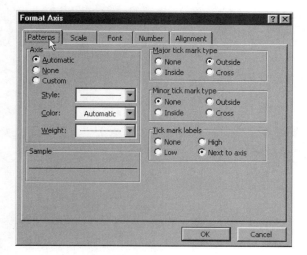

Another editing option is to alter the appearance of the tick marks. Point to and right-click the chart's axis line, then left-click Format on the shortcut menu. Try different options and keep the one that meets your needs.

Folder: 01Descriptive Statistics
Workbook: Making Charts.xls
Worksheet: formatting

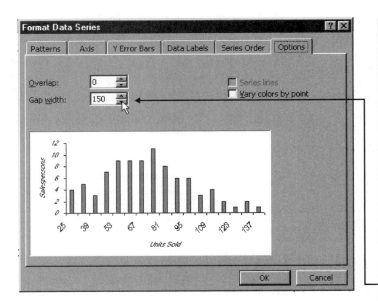

It is usually desirable to widen the histogram bars. In fact, when the variable is continuous rather than categorical (as is the case with these sales data), the convention is to have the bars touch. Point to and right-click one of the bars on the chart. Left-click Format Data Series and this menu will appear.

As you scroll this number to a lower value, the bars will widen.

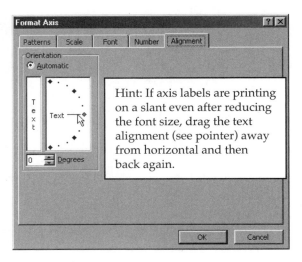

Hint: If axis labels are printing on a slant even after reducing the font size, drag the text alignment (see pointer) away from horizontal and then back again.

Folder: 01 Descriptive Statistics
Workbook: Making Charts.xls
Worksheet: formatting

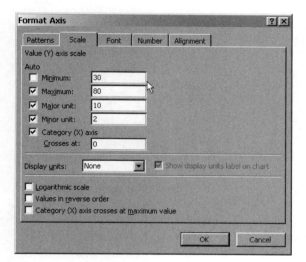

Another useful option on the Format Axis dialog box is for resetting the minimum and maximum of an axis scale. Consider the two line charts below. The one on the left has a good deal of empty space below the data points. By raising the minimum of the axis scale from zero to 30, the whole chart area is used for the display.

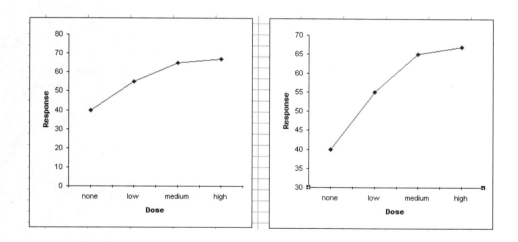

Changing the Minimum to 30 shortens the Y-axis scale, as seen on the right-hand chart above. You will notice that the response now appears to react more sharply to the dose. It is not proper practice to manipulate the scale of a variable simply to create the appearance of an experimental effect. So, use this editing capability with restraint.

CHAPTER 2

The z Statistic

Folder: 02 The z Statistic
Workbook: Comparing Distributions.xls
Worksheet: final grades

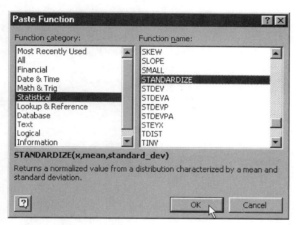

Click the *fx* button to bring up this box. Then select Statistical from the list on the left ("Function category") and STANDARDIZE from the list on the right ("Function name") and click **OK.**

Selecting this cell, invoking the STANDARDIZE paste function, and entering the statistics for the midterm in the dialog box pastes the answer, 1.50, in the cell.

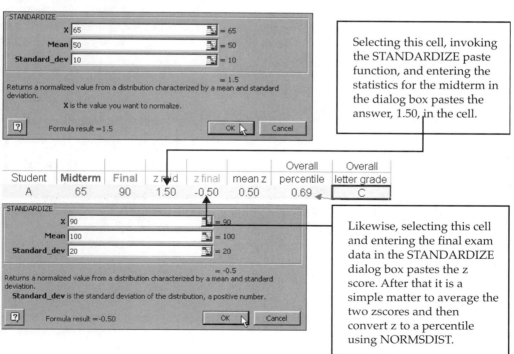

Student	Midterm	Final	z mid	z final	mean z	Overall percentile	Overall letter grade
A	65	90	1.50	-0.50	0.50	0.69	C

Likewise, selecting this cell and entering the final exam data in the STANDARDIZE dialog box pastes the z score. After that it is a simple matter to average the two zscores and then convert z to a percentile using NORMSDIST.

Folder: 02 The z statistic
Workbook: Comparing Distributions.xls
Worksheet: final grades

The formula = (D15+E15)/2 entered in cell F15 adds 1.50
and - 0.50 and divides by 2 to get the student's mean z score.
You may also use the AVERAGE paste function to compute
the mean z score (see box below).

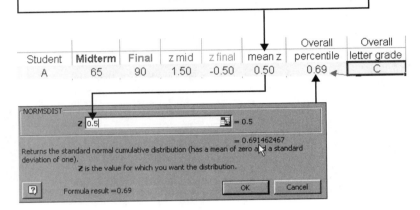

Student	Midterm	Final	z mid	z final	mean z	Overall percentile	Overall letter grade
A	65	90	1.50	-0.50	0.50	0.69	C

NORMSDIST

z | 0.5| = 0.5

= 0.691462467

Returns the standard normal cumulative distribution (has a mean of zero and a standard
deviation of one).

z is the value for which you want the distribution.

Formula result =0.69   OK   Cancel

Student	Midterm	Final	z mid	z final	mean z	Overall percentile	Overall letter grade
A	65	90	1.50	-0.50	0.50	0.69	C

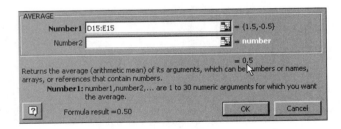

AVERAGE

Number1 | D15:E15   = {1.5,-0.5}
Number2 | = number

= 0.5

Returns the average (arithmetic mean) of its arguments, which can be numbers or names,
arrays, or references that contain numbers.

Number1: number1,number2,... are 1 to 30 numeric arguments for which you want
the average.

Formula result =0.50   OK   Cancel

The AVERAGE paste
function is an alternative
method for computing the
mean of cells D15 and E15
(z mid and z final).

Folder: 02 The z statistic
Workbook: Comparing Distributions
Worksheet: practice

The first step is to determine the mean (AVERAGE) and standard deviation (STDEVP) of the two distributions of examination scores and enter the values in the table for easy reference.

Paste STANDARDIZE here.

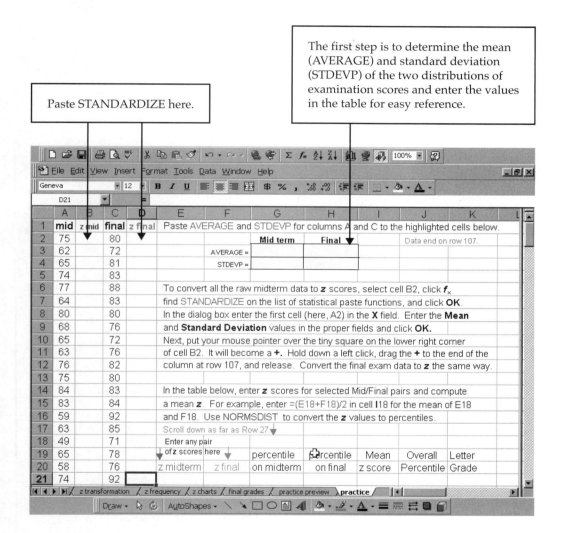

With the means and standard deviations in hand, paste the STANDARDIZE function as instructed, hold down the left mouse button, drag down the length of the column, and release the left mouse button. Excel will copy the STANDARDIZE function to the relevant raw data. With all data converted to z scores, you are ready to complete the grade-assignment exercise.

CHAPTER 3

Correlation and Regression

Folder: 03 Correlation and Regression
Workbook: Type 1 error.xls
Worksheet: exercise

Highlight a random data matrix with a left-click and drag operation. Then, with the mouse pointer over the matrix, right click–Copy. Finally, Paste Special (with Values selected) over the existing matrix in the "my saved data" worksheet. Note that only the numbers are highlighted—no labels.

sample 1	sample 2	sample 3	sample 4	sample 5	sample 6	sample 7	sample 8	sample 9
14	11	10	4	53	45	72	89	99
71	40	65	2	98	20	24	94	60
11	67	4	95	34	36	15	20	48
58	45	12	19	80	68	34	44	45
86	99	85	39	53	3	92	28	77
91	79	16	14	68	69	74	7	41
74	31	79	21	69	43	67	11	45
64	45	78	16	42	10	55	70	25
77	60	41	86	24	29	66	44	3
89	50	5	74	49	16	66	19	57
77	54	49	66	76	38	69	75	40
77	20	54	56	64	9	55	71	40
41	21	91	96	94	19	19	17	28
26	17	13	31	68	3	77	36	80
57	39	92	41	17	32	33	52	28
16	5	43	23	92	11	34	23	96
13	38	96	95	50	10	90	85	21
16	96	59	79	32	30	28	90	70
46	69	23	22	9	55	43	76	16
59	58	16	9	17	32	1	68	2
28	96	79	41	38	56	95	32	24

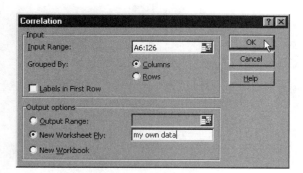

Your Correlation tool dialog box should look like this. The Input Range is from cell A6 to cell I26. Once you click OK the new matrix will appear on a new "my own data" worksheet.

Folder: 03 Correlation and Regression
Workbook: Pearson r.xls
Worksheet: Definitional 2

	A	B	C	D	E	F
1	Pair	X	Y	$(X - \bar{X})^2$	$(Y - \bar{Y})^2$	$(X-\bar{X})(Y-\bar{Y})$
2	A	99	53	2803.70	2.10	-76.78
3	B	60	98			
4	C	48	34			
5	D	45	80			
6	E	77	53			
7	F	41	68			
8	G	45	69			
9	H	25	42			
10	I	3	24			
11	J	57	49			
12	K	40	76			
13	L	40	64			
14	M	28	94			
15	N	80	68			
16	O	28	17			
17	P	96	92			
18	Q	21	50			
19	R	70	32			
20	S	16	9			
21	T	2	17			
22	sums:	921	1089	**2803.70**	**2.10**	**-76.78**

After the drag operation your screen will look like this. The SUM of the column entries appears on line 22. (Be careful not to include line 22 in your drag operation. Stop where the data stops—on line 21.) Repeat a similar drag-to-copy on columns E and F and the solutions for the formula entries will appear in the highlighted cells on the lower right portion of the screen.

The pointer changes to a plus sign when positioned over the tiny box in the lower right corner of the cell. Once the plus sign appears, hold down the left mouse button and drag down the column to the last X-Y pair as shown below.

After the drag operation your screen will look like this. The SUM of the column entries appears on line 22. (Be careful not to include line 22 in your drag operation. Stop where the data stops -- on line 21.) Repeat a similar drag-to-copy on columns E and F and the solutions for the formula entries will appear in the highlighted cells on the lower right portion of the screen.

	A	B	C	D	E	F
1	Pair	X	Y	$(X - \bar{X})^2$	$(Y - \bar{Y})^2$	$(X-\bar{X})(Y-\bar{Y})$
2	A	99	53	2803.70	2.10	-76.78
3	B	60	98	194.60		
4	C	48	34	3.80		
5	D	45	80	1.10		
6	E	77	53	957.90		
7	F	41	68	25.50		
8	G	45	69	1.10		
9	H	25	42	443.10		
10	I	3	24	1853.30		
11	J	57	49	119.90		
12	K	40	76	36.60		
13	L	40	64	36.60		
14	M	28	94	325.80		
15	N	80	68	1152.60		
16	O	28	17	325.80		
17	P	96	92	2495.00		⊕
18	Q	21	50	627.50		
19	R	70	32	573.60		
20	S	16	9	903.00		
21	T	2	17	1940.40		
22	sums:	921	1089	**14820.95**	**2.10**	**-76.78**

Folder: 03 Correlation and Regression
Workbook: Spearman rho.xls
Worksheet: computation

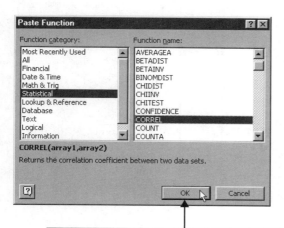

Your paste function dialog box should look like this when accessing the CORREL paste function.

After clicking **OK,** the box below will pop up. Position the mouse pointer over the spreadsheet icon for Array 1 and left click. The dialog box will "roll up" and wait for you to drag the dotted marquee around the data of Array 1 (i.e., the X values).

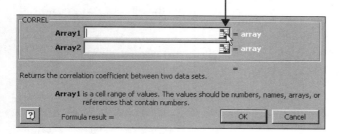

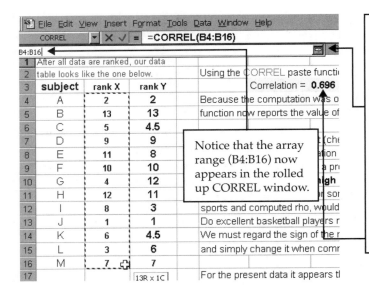

The screen will look like this after you hold the left mouse button down, drag over the X values, and release the mouse button. A click on the icon to the right of the field restores the box to full size and sets you up for entering Array 2 (the Y scores) in the same way. Click **OK** once both arrays are entered and CORREL will paste the answer to the selected cell (here, cell G3).

Notice that the array range (B4:B16) now appears in the rolled up CORREL window.

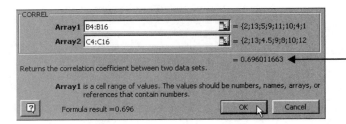

This image shows the CORELL box all filled in and ready, with a click of **OK,** to paste the answer to the selected cell. Notice that the answer to the paste function appears in the box even before clicking **OK.**

Folder: 03 Correlation and Regression
Workbook: Regression.xls
Worksheet: paste functions

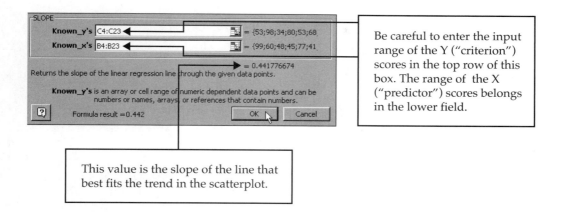

Be careful to enter the input range of the Y ("criterion") scores in the top row of this box. The range of the X ("predictor") scores belongs in the lower field.

This value is the slope of the line that best fits the trend in the scatterplot.

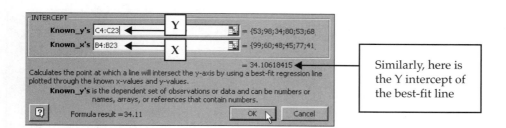

Similarly, here is the Y intercept of the best-fit line

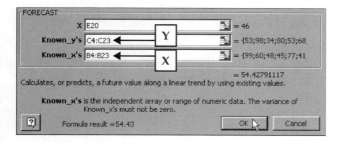

CHAPTER 4

Sampling Distributions

Folder: 04 Sampling Distribution
Workbook: The Binomial.xls
Worksheet: Bernoulli

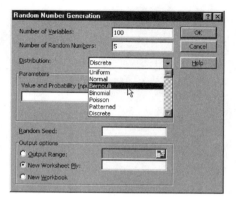

The Random Number generation dialog box will appear once you click the Tools menu, select Random Number Generation, and click **OK.** When you get to the Distribution entry, click the scroll arrow for the Distribution field, then find and click Bernoulli on the list that appears.

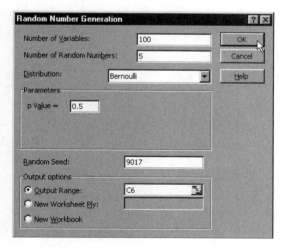

Here is the Random Number Generation dialog box filled in with the appropriate entries. Clicking OK will rerun the Bernoulli experiment for the specific random number entered. Be sure to use a different Random Seed in subsequent reruns. Click **OK** to the warning about overwriting existing data.

Folder: 04 Sampling Distributions
Workbook: The Binomial.xls
Worksheet: Binomial exp

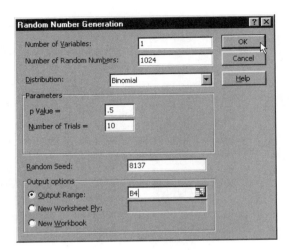

When filled in as shown on the left, the Random Number Generation tool selects 1024 new samples for the binomial sampling experiment in which $n=10$ and $p=.50$.

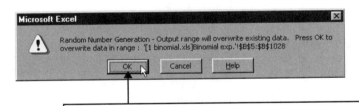

Click **OK** to this warning about overwriting data. After you click **OK** the new data will replace the data that is now on your screen for this experiment.

Folder: 04 Sampling Distributions
Workbook: Central Limit Theorem.xls
Worksheet: your data (*n* = 9)

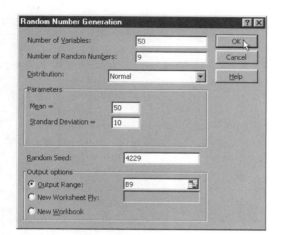

This experiment selects 50 samples (*n*=9 per sample) from a population in which μ=50, σ=10.

Click the Format drop-down menu and click Cells as the first step to reformat the highlighted data.

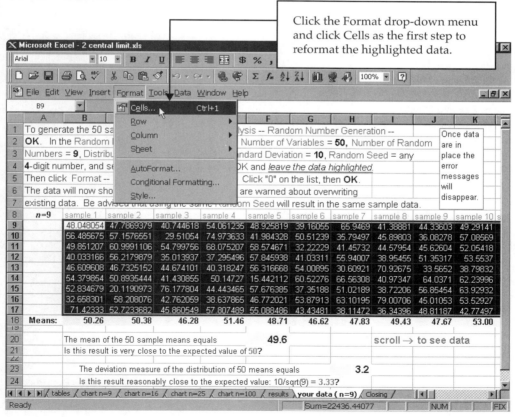

CHAPTER 5

Probability

Folder: 05 Probability
Workbook: Computing Probability
Worksheets: exact / X or fewer / X or more

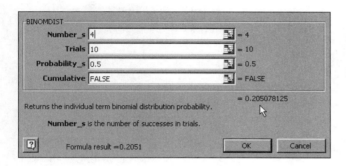

With these values entered into the four fields, the BINOMDIST paste function outputs the probability of *exactly* 4 successes in 10 trials when p(success) =.50.

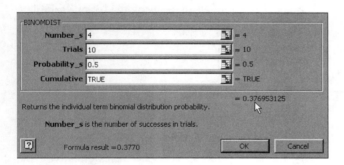

By changing the FALSE entry to TRUE, the BINOMDIST paste function outputs the probability of *4 or fewer* successes in 10 trials when p(success) =.50

The probability of 4 or more successes is the same as (1 minus the probability of 3 or fewer successes. Here, the result (.172) is for 3 or fewer successes. So, the probability of 4 or more successes equals 1 - .172 = **.828**.

Folder: 05 Probability
Workbook: Computing Probability
Worksheet: =, < or =

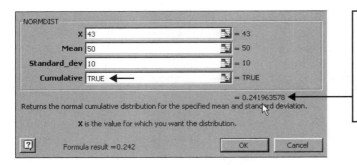

NORMDIST tells us that
the probability of selecting
a random value from the
population (μ=50, σ=10)
that is *less than or equal to*
43 equals .24 .

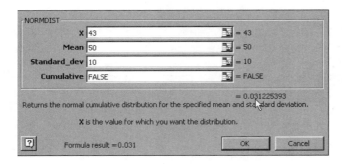

By entering FALSE in the
Cumulative field,
NORMDIST outputs the
probability (.03) of a sample
that equals *exactly* 43.

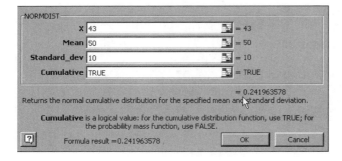

Because the Cumulative
= TRUE specification
causes NORMDIST to
output a proportion of
area equal to or less than
X, to find 43 *or more* we
must compute 1 minus
p(X or less). Here, the
answer is **1-.24 = .76**.

CHAPTER 6

The *t* Statistic—One Sample

Folder: 06 The *t* Statistic—One Sample
Workbook: Estimating Error
Worksheet: experiment

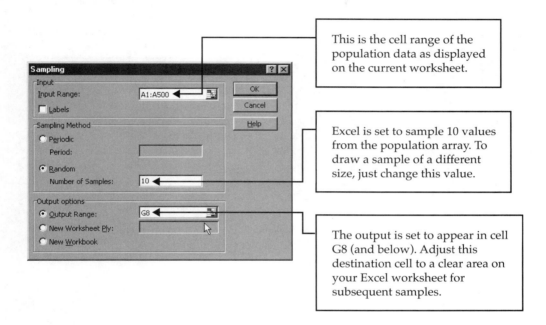

This is the cell range of the population data as displayed on the current worksheet.

Excel is set to sample 10 values from the population array. To draw a sample of a different size, just change this value.

The output is set to appear in cell G8 (and below). Adjust this destination cell to a clear area on your Excel worksheet for subsequent samples.

The AVERAGE, STDEV, and STDEVP dialog boxes are virtually the same. The only field to fill in (Number 1) is the range of cells that hold the data on which you wish the function to operate.

Folder: 06 The *t* Statistic—One Sample
Workbook: Rationale of the *t* Test
Worksheet: experiment / t formula

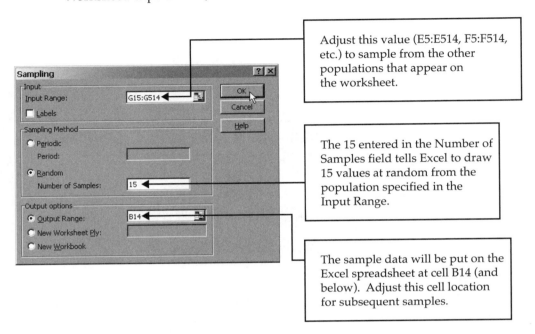

Adjust this value (E5:E514, F5:F514, etc.) to sample from the other populations that appear on the worksheet.

The 15 entered in the Number of Samples field tells Excel to draw 15 values at random from the population specified in the Input Range.

The sample data will be put on the Excel spreadsheet at cell B14 (and below). Adjust this cell location for subsequent samples.

This is the range of cells that hold the sample data.

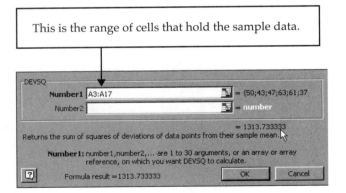

Folder: 06 The *t* Statistic—One Sample
Workbook: Confidence Intervals.xls
Worksheet: demo2

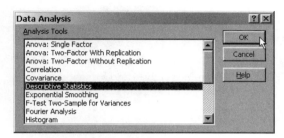

As usual, the first step in running a data analysis tool is to access the Data Analysis menu from the Tools drop-down menu. Find Descriptive Statistics on the list and click **OK**.

This is the input range of the sample data.

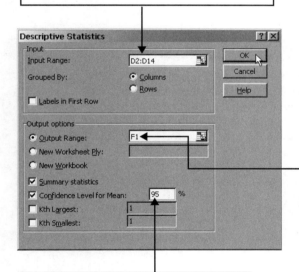

The Descriptive Statistics dialog box should look like this on the demo2 worksheet. The entries may automatically change to include $ symbols (such as $D$2:$D$14) before you get to click **OK**. This is not a problem.

The worksheet is already set up to receive the output of the Descriptive Statistics tool in cell F1 (and below). When working on your own with this tool you will have to make the columns wider for full viewing (See basic skills.xls for a complete description of the "drag to widen" procedure).

To compute a 99% confidence interval, change this entry to 99.

Folder: 06 The *t* Statistic—One Sample
Workbook: Confidence Intervals.xls
Worksheet: exercise 1

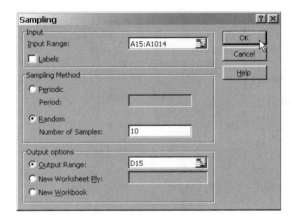

The entries in this Sampling tool dialog box allow Excel to take a sample of 10 values from a 1000-score population and locate the sample data in cell D15.

sample data
64
59
72
61
93
63
72
52
80
75

Holding a left click while dragging down the sample array will highlight the data. With your mouse pointer within the highlighted area, right click and select Copy from the shortcut menu (in preparation for Pasting on the next worksheet.

Folder: 06 The *t* Statistic—One Sample
Workbook: Confidence Intervals
Worksheet: exercise 1

To generate new population data using the Random Number Generation tool:
Click Tools–Data Analysis–Random Number Generation–**OK**. In the
Random Number Generation dialog box, set Number of Variables = 1, Number of Random
Numbers = the number of values you wish to be in your population. Set Distribution to Normal,
Mean = your chosen value for μ, Standard Deviation = your chosen SD value, and
Random Seed = any 4-digit number. Set Output Range to A15, the location of the first cell of
population data.

Click **OK** and leave the data highlighted. Then click Format–Cells–Number tab–Custom.
Click "0" on the list, then **OK**. The population data will now show as integers.

Be advised that using the same Random Seed will result in the same data.

Once you have the population in place, click Tools–Sampling–**OK** to collect sample data.
The Input Range spans the population data array you generated in column A
For example, if you elected to have 100 values in the population, you would enter A15:A114 .
After selecting Random, let Number of Random Numbers equal your chosen sample size.
The Output Range = the cell under the sample column heading (D15).
If you wish the data to display as integers use the same procedure described above
(leave the data highlighted etc. . . .)

Folder: The t Statistic - One Sample
Workbook: Confidence Intervals.xls
Worksheet: sampling experiment

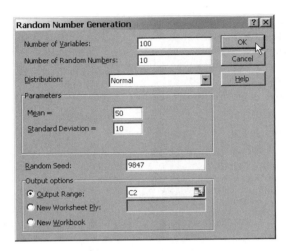

This image shows the dialog box entries you need for repeating the experiment on the "sampling experiment" worksheet. Be sure to use a new random seed for each subsequent repetition. The other entries need not be changed.

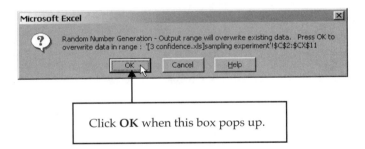

Click **OK** when this box pops up.

Folder: 06 The t Statistic - One Sample
Workbook: Confidence Intervals.xls
Worksheet: sampling experiment

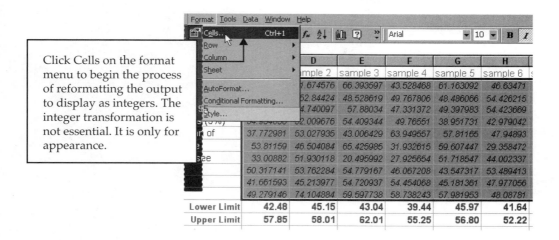

Click Cells on the format menu to begin the process of reformatting the output to display as integers. The integer transformation is not essential. It is only for appearance.

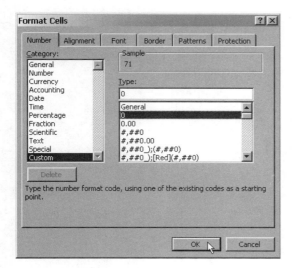

Once you click Cell on the Format drop-down menu this menu appears. Click the Number tab at the top, select Custom from the list on the left and 0 from the list on the right, then **OK**. The new sample data will then display as integers.

CHAPTER 7

The *t* Statistic—Two Samples

Folder: The *t* Statistic—Two Samples
Workbook: Estimating Error.xls
Worksheet: experiment

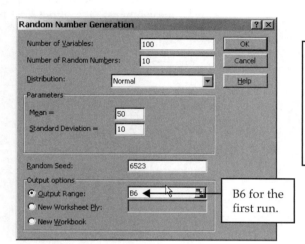

This box shows the entries in the Random Number Generation dialog box for generating the first set of sample data. In subsequent reruns you need only change the Random Seed. The other entries remain the same.

B6 for the first run.

After clicking OK you will see a warning about overwriting data. Click **OK** to continue.

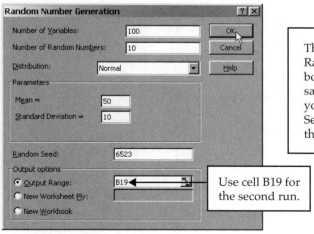

This box shows the entries in the Random Number Generation dialog box for generating the second set of sample data. In subsequent reruns you need only change the Random Seed. The other entries remain the same.

Use cell B19 for the second run.

Folder: The *t* Statistic—Two Samples
Workbook: Independent versus Related.xls
Worksheet: DEVSQ

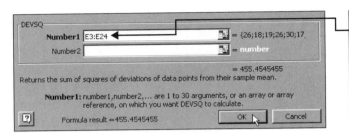

This entry in the DEVSQ paste function dialog box computes the SStotal for the combined set (sample 1 and sample 2) of 22 data values.

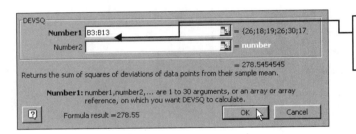

This entry computes the SS within sample 1.

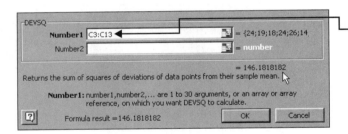

Likewise, here is the entry for computing the SS within sample 2.

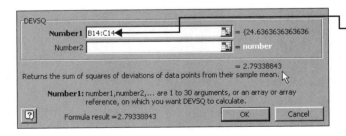

This is the DEVSQ function applied to the two sample *means*. We have to multiply the answer, **2.793**, by *n* (here, *n*=11) to express the DEVSQ result (the SSbetween) in terms of raw scores.

CHAPTER 8

Single-Factor ANOVA

Folder: 08 Single-factor ANOVA
Workbook: The ANOVA Model.xls
Worksheet: demo

The first step in sampling new data is to highlight the existing data matrix. Position the mouse pointer over the cell in the top left corner. Then, while holding a left click on your mouse, drag the mouse pointer to the cell in the bottom right corner and let go of the mouse button.

With the mouse pointer over the highlighted area, right click to access the shortcut menu. Click Clear Contents. This will restore blank cells to the data array in preparation for your new data.

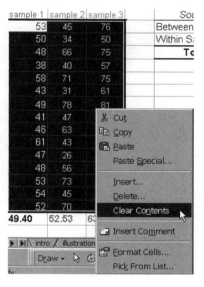

Worksheet: demo (continued...)

This Input Range directs Excel to draw the sample data from the population in column N. Change the Input range to O3:O502 or P3:P502 to select data from the other two populations.

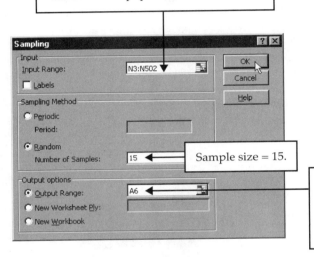

Sample size = 15.

This sample data will locate in cell A6. For the other two samples, change this entry to B6 or C6.

Folder: 08 Single-Factor ANOVA
Workbook: The ANOVA Model
Worksheet: effect size and variability

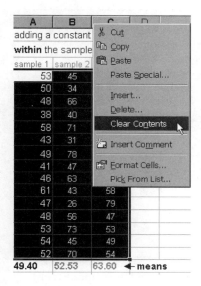

You may type over existing data values, but if you wish to draw new sample data from the populations, start off by clearing the existing data. Highlight the data with a left click and drag operation. Then, with your mouse pointer over the highlighted area, right click and select clear contents from the shortcut menu. Ignore error messages on the display. They will disappear once all the new data are in place.

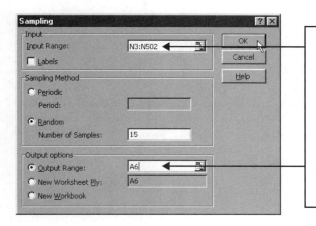

There are three populations from which to draw data. They are located in worksheet columns N, O, and P. The entry in the Input range field tells Excel the range of the population from which to draw the sample. Here, the box is set up to draw a sample of **15** values from the population in column N and put the data in cell **A6**.

Worksheet: effect size and variability (continued…)

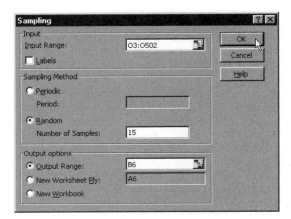

The entries in this Sampling tool dialog box direct Excel to select 15 values at random from the population in column O and place the data in cell B6. As shown, leave the Number of Samples at 15.

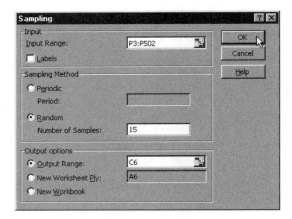

The final run of the Sampling tool draws the new data from the population in column P and places the data in cell C6, thus completing the data replacement procedure. With the three new samples in place, the ANOVA, means, and chart will show the analysis of the new data.

Folder: 08 Single-Factor ANOVA
Workbook: The ANOVA Model
Worksheet: your sample size

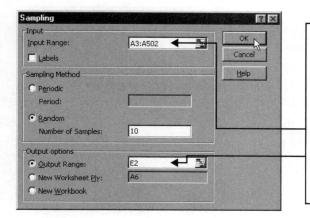

This Sampling tool dialog box directs Excel to select 10 values from the population in column A and then place the values in cell E2. To sample from the other populations simply change the Input Range to **B3:B502** or **C3:C502** and change the Output Range to **F3** or **G3**. Once the sample data are in place, run the Anova: Single Factor tool.

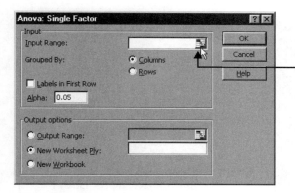

The first step in running the Anova: Single Factor tool is to set the Input Range. Click the spreadsheet icon. The dialog box will roll up like a window shade in preparation for the next step.

Worksheet: your sample size (continued…)

E	F	G
sample 1	sample 2	sample 3
42	53	61
48	62	46
47	49	72
70	58	69
53	47	51
56	80	69
33	48	60
58	76	46
47	82	48
51	50	61

The next step is to point to the top left cell in the data array, hold down the left mouse button, drag to the cell in the lower right of the array, and let go of the mouse button. A dotted marquee will surround the data as shown here. Cell E2 will always be the first in the Input Range, but the end of the Input Range (the lower right cell) will change as your sample size changes.

The Input Range (the cells within the dotted marquee) will show in the Anova: Single Factor dialog box. Click the spreadsheet icon again and the dialog box will unroll to its full size.

Anova: Single Factor
$E$2:$G$11

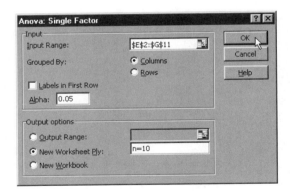

It is best to put the ANOVA results on a new worksheet with a name that indicates your choice of sample size. Here, because this illustration uses $n=10$, the new worksheet is named "n=10." When you click OK, Excel will create the new "n=10" worksheet, place the output on that worksheet, and display the worksheet on your screen. As usual, you will have to widen columns to view the full contents of the ANOVA table.

CHAPTER 9

Two-Factor ANOVA

Folder: 09 Two-Factor ANOVA
Workbook: Interpreting ANOVA Results.xls
Worksheet: your sample data

This entry stays the same
for all sample selections.

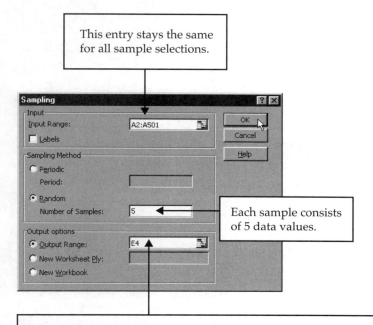

Each sample consists
of 5 data values.

The Output Range will take one of eight values, depending on which cell in the
data matrix is designated to hold the new data. Moving in the top section of the
2 x 4 matrix (One-on-one Therapy) from left to right, the entries are E4 (shown
here), F4, G4, and H4. To replace the data in the cells of the lower section (Group
Therapy), use the entries E9, F9, G9, or H9.

Folder: 09 Two-Factor ANOVA
Workbook: Computational Method.xls
Worksheet: demo data set

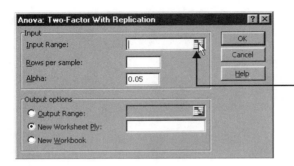

Click the Tools drop-down menu, then select Anova: Two-Factor With Replication. Click the spreadsheet icon as shown to se the Input Range with a drag operation.

After clicking the icon, the window will roll up like a window shade.

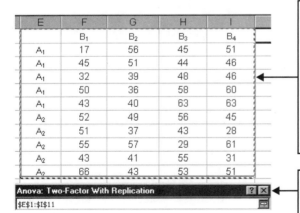

E	F	G	H	I
	B₁	B₂	B₃	B₄
A₁	17	56	45	51
A₁	45	51	44	46
A₁	32	39	48	46
A₁	50	36	58	60
A₁	43	40	63	63
A₂	52	49	56	45
A₂	51	37	43	28
A₂	55	57	29	61
A₂	43	41	55	31
A₂	66	43	53	51

Point to the top left cell (E1), and with the left mouse button depressed, drag to the lower right corner and release the mouse button. You should see the dotted marquee overlapping the red lines. The Input Range information will appear in the window of the Anova tool, which is still "rolled up".

Anova: Two-Factor With Replication
$E$1:$I$11

Click the icon again to restore the dialog box (see next image).

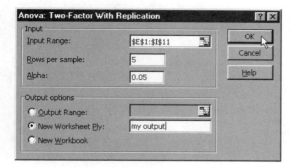

With the Input Range entered all that remains is to enter the "Rows per sample" (i.e., the number of values per cell), the alpha level (usually .05), and an Output Range. A new worksheet has been selected for the Output Range called "my output." Once you click **OK**, Excel will do the analysis and put the results on the new worksheet. Click in a blank area of the worksheet and widen the columns as necessary to view the output properly.